SPITFIRE

A Story of
Adversity, Acceptance and Resurrection

Leslie C. Smith

Green Heart Living Press

Spitfire: A Story of Adversity, Acceptance and Resurrection

Copyright © 2023 Leslie C. Smith

All rights reserved. No part of this book may be used or reproduced by any means, graphic, electronic, or mechanical, including photocopying, recording, taping or by any information storage retrieval system without the written permission of the publisher, except in the case of brief quotations embodied in critical articles and reviews.

ISBN Paperback: 9781954493391

Cover design: Elizabeth B. Hill

This book is designed to provide information and motivation to our readers. It is sold with the understanding that the publisher is not engaged to render any type of psychological, legal, or any other kind of professional advice. The content of each article is the sole expression and opinion of its author, and not necessarily that of the publisher. No warranties or guarantees are expressed or implied by the publisher's choice to include any of the content in this volume. Neither the publisher nor the author shall be liable for any physical, psychological, emotional, financial, or commercial damages, including, but not limited to, special, incidental, consequential or other damages. Our views and rights are the same: You are responsible for your own choices, actions, and results.

Dedication

To my father Harvey C. Smith,
who gave me life, unwavering support and
unconditional love.

Contents

Foreword	7
Preface	9

Part One: Coin Toss

Disaster Strikes	15
Destruction	21
Spitfire	25
My Element	29

Part Two: Grip

Grip	33
Athlete At Heart	37
Applying To College	45
Incipit Vita Nova	47
Regaining Grip	49
Grip With Both Hands	51
Strengthening Grip	53

Part Three: Love

Love	57
Marriage	59
40-love/ love-40	65
6-0, 6-0	69
Heartbreak	71
My Wish	79
High Heels	81
Pleiotropy	85
What You Can Expect	89
Tilt	95

Part Four: Serving and Receiving Serve

Family Relationships	109
Delayed Adolescence	115
Invisible Disability	117
Take Fair Out of the Dictionary	121
Maybe You're Just Lazy	125

Part Five: Singles

Singles	129
Alone	133
My Place	139
Being Thankful	143

Part Six: Two Bounces

Two Bounces	147
Helping Hand	151
Learning The Basics	157
Basic Training	161
Become One with The Chair	163
Tournaments	167
Competitive Edge	169

Part Seven: Deuce

Deuce	173
Positive & Competitive	175
Empathy & Compassion	177
Passion	181
Hope & Faith	183
Joy	185
Transition	189
Moving Forward	193

Conclusion	195
Epilogue	197
Appendix	199
About the Author	201

Foreword

My world first collided with Leslie's in 1994 at the start of our freshman year at Scripps College in Claremont, California. We were dormmates and we became instant friends. She was an expert tennis player, a trait which landed her on our school's tennis team, but she likewise had a knack for any sport she picked up. When I met her mother a few months later I came to understand where she got her grit.

When I met her father, I knew where she got her non-judgmental concern for people. Then, as now, she naturally gave others an immediate benefit of the doubt. Thus, I knew I could always be my authentic self around her. For that gift I am forever grateful; I avail myself of it to this day. In the summer before our last year of college, we backpacked through Europe. Each morning we would wake up with grand plans to spend the entire day touring ancient cities, but Leslie would inevitably tire out halfway through the day. I did not understand how an athlete of her caliber could be so easily drained. In hindsight, our trip brought into focus what was actually an ongoing, gradual waning of her initial energy levels over the course of our four years together; her radiant presence was increasingly dampened by low-hanging clouds, the genesis of which was unknown to us at the time.

When I learned of Leslie's diagnosis, I was a graduate student studying genetic counseling. I have been struck by these types of coincidences and connections that we have. I was learning about the complexities of inherited disorders just as Leslie was learning about her own family's condition.

Myotonic Muscular Dystrophy (MMD) is a complex condition characterized by some of the most complicated genetic concepts. The most common symptoms are progressive muscle loss and weakness, myotonia, which is an impaired ability to relax muscles, and abnormal heart rhythms. MMD is in a category of genetic conditions called trinucleotide repeat disorders. Nucleotides are the building blocks of DNA, and a "trinucleotide" is a set of three nucleotides. Many genes have repetitive regions, but when there are too many repetitions, the gene coding gets disrupted, leading to clinical symptoms. MMD is also characterized by "anticipation," a phenomenon that occurs because these repeats tend to become longer with each passing generation, leading to earlier onset and more severe disease. One of the characteristics of MMD that is vividly present in Leslie's family is pleiotropy in which disruption of a single gene can lead to multiple, seemingly unrelated symptoms.

Through Leslie's recounting, you will see how each of these medical terms translates into real-life impact. How would she take the news that she inherited a condition that would not only lead to a shortened lifespan but would also slowly eat away at her muscles—the very thing that has defined her youth? How would she take the news that her father's life was likely nearing an end? What would this mean for her brother? What would this mean for her mother, whose three family members could be ripped away from her? How does someone whose youth and sense of self-worth that is so dependent upon her independence, athleticism, and physical capabilities navigate through the news that, over time, her muscles will deteriorate, that her energy level will wane, and she will become increasingly reliant on the assistance of others?

Leslie's is a story of triumph, perseverance, and passion for life—a lesson for all of us. You will see how she reconciles these losses and emerges on the other side. She learned to love life again and to love herself again, with the same passion and fervor that she loves those around her.

Kelly Farwell Hagman, MS, CGC
Genetic Counselor
Senior Director of Medical Affairs at Ambry Genetics

Preface

The Oncoming Train
2011

I was moving the clothes from the washer to the dryer in the basement of my mother's house when I felt a wave of dizziness crest over me. Had I stayed in bed too long? Was it the Diet Coke I'd been drinking? Maybe I hadn't eaten enough? Or perhaps this was just me not feeling well and getting dizzy, as I sometimes do. Typically, when this happened, my response was to wait it out. But this didn't feel like ordinary light-headedness. It was far more intense.

I'd been advised to sit down if I ever felt woozy. I sank to the floor, blackness closing in around me. I was unconscious. The next thing I knew, a freight train was heading straight toward me, headlight blinding in the pitch dark. Then I felt a powerful jolt to my body, strong enough to jerk me back to consciousness. I could feel the cold concrete floor beneath me, and as I opened my eyes, I could see the side of the washing machine. I was lying on my side, but why? I recalled feeling dizzy and then the freight train. Now what I felt was panic. What had just happened to me? A sudden pain in my chest told me everything I needed to know. My defibrillator had just fired.

The first call I made was to my husband, Rob. Please come, I begged him through my tears. The next call was to my mother, who was currently three thousand miles away in California with my dad and brother and not scheduled to return for at least two months. I'd barely finished telling my mother what happened before she'd gone into what I'd come to think of as her "rallying the troops" mode. The minute we were off the phone, she phoned my godmother and asked her to accompany my husband, then called a neighbor to come and sit with me while the others were on their way.

"Are you sitting down?" my mother asked when she called back a few minutes later to share this information with me.

"I had to get up to answer the phone," I said, reminding her that the antiquated rotary phone that she'd just called me on was obviously not cordless.

While I was feeling a little better, I was still freaked out about what had just happened. My defibrillator had fired once before but it hadn't been anything like this. Fortunately, when Rob arrived, he'd brought not just my godmother but my portable heart monitor. That meant that I could send a transmission to my cardiologist who could then read the activity on my defibrillator. It was handy that my husband was training to be an ER nurse and was a natural caretaker.

After checking in with my doctors in Vermont and Baltimore, I was given the choice of heading directly to the hospital or waiting until the morning. In the meantime, the on-call doctor looked at the transmission and put a name to what had happened to me: ventricular tachycardia. It's a kind of arrhythmia that will kill you in a few short moments if you don't have an implantable cardioverter defibrillator (ICD). It was the arrhythmia that had caused me to pass out, the firing of the ICD then jolting me back to consciousness. The doctor assured us that it was fine for me to stay home, but if this happened again, we'd have to call 911 to transport me to the hospital.

Since it was Sunday night, I overruled my assisting entourage and voted to just go home. Rob and I drove directly there. I made it out of the car and up the stairs to our front door when that same feeling of intense dizziness washed over me. I sunk to the porch.

The next thing I heard was Rob shouting my name: "Leslie! Leslie!" When he saw me slumped against the front door, he thought I was dead. He'd later tell me that of all we'd been through together, this was by far the saddest, scariest time of all. He'd thought he'd lost me.

Lost to the black fog of unconsciousness, I couldn't hear him. I had no idea where I was, just that the same awful, blinding headlight of the train was back. Racing toward me out of the darkness, it was shining directly at me and getting closer by the second.

People who've had near-death experiences often talk about "seeing the light"—a heavenly glow that makes them feel warm, safe and protected. This light was nothing like that. Instead of feeling blissful, I was immobilized by stark terror and a sense of impending doom. Unable to speak or move, and with no knowledge of what was happening around me, all I could do was lie there as the train bore down on me.

As I struggled back to consciousness, I managed to choke out a single word, more moan than speech. The word was "Mama."

Tennis...Again
2017

I was finally about to play tennis again. I had heard about a clinic that happened every Saturday, in New Hampshire. In October of 2017, with quite a bit of trepidation, mixed with excitement, I went to check it out.

It had been years and I couldn't wait to immerse myself in my favorite sport. I'd had a few lessons to dust off my skills and replace my outdated equipment. Walking into the Y, carrying all my tennis paraphernalia I felt my heartbeat speed up. I have always loved everything about tennis and was so excited about the opportunity to rejoin the sport. As I got on the court to do drills, I reveled in the sight of the crisp white lines on the courts and of players glowing with sweat after a satisfying game, and most of all, the smell of new tennis balls. I was swinging my racket in anticipation of a hard workout. I couldn't wait to start hitting and reclaim the athlete I had once been. I remembered the feeling of hitting the crap out of the ball, the sound the ball made when it connected with the sweet spot of the racket and the thrill of hitting an amazing shot.

I got ready to take my turn as the drill was explained. I felt all the old skills coming back. Moving into position I set up for a forehand. I hit the ball and smiled, feeling the pleasant surge of muscles in my arm. I continued focusing on moving to the ball, hitting a good shot and getting the dust off my rusty skills.

It was just like I had remembered...except this time I was playing in a wheelchair.

PART ONE

COIN TOSS

DISASTER STRIKES
Age 24 Pre-Diagnosis

In the back of my mind, I had known for several years that something was amiss, not only with my own health but with the health of my brother and father too. I never thought we were all suffering from the same condition as our symptoms were so varied. The only symptom we seemed to have in common was fatigue.

Around this time, I was going through a bookshelf at our summer cottage looking for something to read. I came across a book that had a notecard in it. I recognized my mother's handwriting. Through reading a book by Carolyn Myss she came to believe that my father, my brother Colin, and I all had a fatigue disorder.

I had just always figured my dad's struggle could be attributed to the fact that he was getting older, I was just tired in general, and my brother was always pretty much a mystery.

Colin never wondered what his number would be. Myotonic Muscular Dystrophy (MMD) Type one is caused by having too many of what are known as "trinucleotide repeats" in the DMN1 gene on chromosome 19. Nucleotides are the building blocks of DNA, and a "trinucleotide" is a set of three nucleotides. Many genes have repetitive regions, but when there are too many repetitions, the gene coding gets disrupted, and the clinical symptoms result. Genetic testing can reveal how many of these repeats a person has. Since the symptoms of MMD manifest differently in everyone, the number of repeats can be a general indication of the disease severity; however, it does not denote how the disease will progress or what symptoms you will have and when. Trinucleotide repeat disorders are associated with what is known as "anticipation." This is a phenomenon in which symptoms get more severe with each generation. The underlying reason for the increasing severity is because the DNA repeat length tends to get longer in each passing generation. The number differentiates between the different onsets of MMD: Late-onset, symptoms emerging later in life, repeats are between 50-100, adolescent/adult or classic, onset in teenage years with repeats from 150-1000, and congenital which is usually over 10,000.

While all three of us have been genetically tested, only my father and I decided to get the results. The tests revealed that my father had 96 repeats and I had 594, which stands to reason, as his symptoms developed later in life while mine manifested in early adulthood. With each generation the number of repeats tends to expand, leading to more severe disease per generation. Since my brother and I both had adolescent onset, it would stand to reason that his number would be similar to mine.

When asked why he won't get his genetic testing results his response is that he already knows that he has the disease and there is no reason to find out his number of repeats, as it is irrelevant. Once you get your number it is not something you will ever forget, after you receive it there is no going back. In Colin's case it may be much more beneficial for him not to know it.

In the end, getting his results might have a negative result. Since there is a large range of repeat numbers, there is concern that if his number were higher than mine it might be seen as his situation being worse than mine, or him needing more support. Which is, in fact, the case. And darn it, he would not get tested just to satisfy his sister's curiosity.

In many ways, both my brother and I having inherited MMD can almost be seen as a positive. It was clear for several years that something was going on that had affected both of us as well as my father but had this not been the case, I think our family would have become more divided. This way, theoretically, we can support each other and be bonded by an understanding that no one else can. Even though we see my mother all the time and she witnessed my father's struggles, she can only sympathize with what we experience. It is impossible for anyone to really understand what and how you feel. They can see the effects, bear daily witness, understand intellectually, but no one who doesn't have the disease can really understand it. It has always been so important to me for people to understand. People say, "I can imagine what you are going through," but I know that no one really does.

    I was diagnosed in October of 2000 when I was 25 years old. In some ways, this was a relief, as I knew something was wrong with me. For the past three years, I had been on a quest to determine where all the symptoms that I was experiencing came from. I didn't feel like a "normal" 22-year-old. I was tired all the time, I couldn't keep up with my friends, and had spent most of my senior year of college in bed. I repeatedly went to the doctor, was given a blood test and assured nothing was wrong with me, other than a slightly elevated cholesterol level. After being assured that all the symptoms I had discussed were in my head, I was given pamphlets on how to lower my cholesterol and was sent on my way. Not caring about my cholesterol, I left the pamphlets in the car and decided to try another route.

    I started seeing a Naturopath, who diagnosed me with chronic fatigue, Epstein Barr, and a variety of other ailments. The treatments for these maladies did nothing for me, and I continued my search. My father had joined in my crusade for answers as he, at 64, had experienced an extreme drop in energy and stamina. We both knew something was wrong but had relatively little idea what. Our expectation was that eventually, what was going on would be diagnosed, we would be given treatment, and all would be fine.

    One day, my father finally received a diagnosis. I will never forget the day he told me. Both my father and I were in Gloucester at my parent's cottage on the ocean. It was a beautiful, sunny summer day, and I could hear the surf and see the seagulls flying above. My dad asked me to take a walk on the beach with him, an unexpected treat. It was late in the afternoon and avoiding anyone we knew; we went to sit down by the water's edge. I knew something was up but was so happy to be with my dad at the beach that I wasn't really frightened.

    My dad told me that he wanted to have a private conversation, but I saw no reason to be worried and was convinced that there was nothing he could say that would dampen this beautiful day. Also, my dad has always tried to make unpleasant or difficult situations easier for me if possible.

As we sat at the water's edge, my dad looked at me. I smiled back, trying to put him at ease.

My father's face looked peaceful a
nd there was nothing worried or panicked in his voice. Feeling the warm sun on my shoulders, watching the waves roll into shore I was happy as I listened to my dad and sifted the soft sand through my fingers.

"You know that I've been having some trouble with fatigue and am lately having trouble with swallowing. I've been meeting with the doctor to try and determine why this is occurring."

I knew my dad had been meeting with his GP and several specialists and had been given several different diagnoses, including ALS. Getting a feeling that this conversation wasn't going to be very pleasant I continued trying to smile at my dad as he went on.

"After several false diagnoses, I've been diagnosed with Muscular Dystrophy. We don't really know what that means but it may explain the symptoms I've been having."

I must have shown my puzzlement. I had never really heard about MD. It wasn't on my radar at all. I knew this couldn't be a good thing but had no idea of what the ramifications would be or what this would come to mean to me.

"How is it diagnosed?" I asked my father.

"There are some blood tests they can do to determine if you have the altered gene, and there are some identifying traits. It's certain that I have it. I'm not telling you to scare you, but the Doctor is pretty sure your brother has it as well. Mom and I are going to tell him this weekend and we wanted you to know ahead of time."

He still didn't give me much of an explanation of what this diagnosis meant and I assumed it was fairly benign. He must have mentioned it was hereditary. My parents were sure that the disclosure to my brother would be met by firm denial, as denial is one of my brother's closest bedfellows. They were telling me in advance so that I could be helpful and supportive with the fallout.

I remember smiling at my dad as we continued to sit on the beach and to try and make him smile and laugh as well. I use humor as a coping mechanism and try to lighten the mood using my dry sense of humor. This still seemed like such a minor thing to me and nothing to get all upset about.

I was astounded months later when I realized that the most obvious person to have it would be me, as my dad and I are carbon copies in many ways. I didn't bear any of the symptoms or signs at that point other than fatigue, which I figured could be attributed to any number of things, but nothing very serious.

Although my brother was diagnosed by sight, due to the facial markers he exhibited, I had to have a needle stuck into my hand muscle to determine if the enzymes that are released by muscle deterioration were present. As we sat in the first of many neurologist's office and received our official diagnosis, he cautioned us to get an education, so we never had to make our living by our backs. He only gave us the broadest overview of what we could expect, wheelchairs being the only one that registered and overall, I don't remember being that upset or frightened. In some part, we had finally received the diagnosis that we had all been looking for, for a long time. It was assumed that this was the simple answer to all the questions, but at the time I didn't understand that the symptoms we were experiencing were the tip of the iceberg. My brother had gotten perhaps more details and had a greater understanding of the ramifications and was more upset than I was.

After all, I felt fine, if a little tired, which seemed to be a hopeful sign and I was not too discouraged. A little denial can be quite helpful at times. Of course, I had a total lack of understanding of what I was facing. That would come later.

Although my brother and I were told at different places, it was a situation of, as Dickens would say, the best of times and the worst of times. Going for a walk on the beach with my dad was an unexpected treat. What I took away from it most of all was that my father wanted my support when they told my brother. For my brother, especially since they were pretty sure he had inherited it, it was much more distressing.

He was sitting on the sun porch, a favorite spot, looking out over the ocean, which leads you to feel a sense of safety, happiness, and peace. Perhaps being in such a wonderful place lessened the blow of the news he received. What I didn't realize at the time was the incredible feeling of guilt and devastation from my father, thinking that he had passed this on to at least one, if not both, of his children. For my mother, the terrible blow of potentially her three family members being diagnosed with a life-altering, incurable disease was shattering.

DESTRUCTION

Two months after we received our diagnosis from the neurologist in Middlebury, we went to the Muscular Dystrophy Clinic in Burlington. My parents picked me up from work, and I was in a great mood. I'd had a good day and was looking forward to going out to dinner after our doctor's appointment. I was a single, lively, 25-year-old woman who enjoyed every moment of my life. I had recently lost a lot of weight and was wearing a new outfit that looked awesome. I had on a purple cashmere sweater, a short black skirt, tights, and cute shoes. I'd borrowed my mother's leather jacket and I can recall sitting in the waiting room, feeling happy and sexy and joking around with my brother. I felt neither fear nor anxiety. Why would I? As far as I knew, this was just a routine doctor's visit.

Things began to change very quickly.

We were each put into an exam room and left alone for what seemed like a long time. I remember wishing that I'd brought a book and hoping that I wouldn't have to take my tights off. Eventually, a doctor came in. He was young, and I hoped that we'd be able to establish some sort of rapport. I don't remember much about what he said, except that his questions seemed random, and his tone implied that he was not one to be trifled with. My attempts at humor were not appreciated. And it went downhill from there.

To offset some of the symptoms my dad and I were experiencing, we'd started a regimen of supplements and vitamin IVs. When I tried to describe this to the doctor who was "examining" me, he looked at me like I was crazy. It was clear that he had no idea what I was talking about, and I felt immediately judged. And that was the most positive part of the interaction.

Once our respective examinations were complete, my family reunited in a conference room, as the doctors conferred in whispers at the other end of the table. Without asking so much as a single question, they'd reached their conclusion. It was time for the diagnosis.

Spitfire

I can still feel the anger and despair I experienced that day as though I was right back in that clinic. Did I mention that I was angry? If there is one thing that I cannot stand, it is being condescended to. When someone looks down on me it positively makes my blood boil. I feel utterly helpless and as if my life doesn't matter. My reaction is usually to respond with extreme rudeness and sarcasm, which makes me feel better but doesn't tend to help the situation.

Perhaps somebody had told me that one of them was the head of the MD clinic, the other his underling. I don't remember knowing or caring. All I knew was that of all the doctors I had met thus far; these two had the worst bedside manner. They were apparently very important, at least they clearly thought they were. Although one was clearly the more senior of the two, they seemed, to me at least, to be somewhat interchangeable, each with a no-nonsense appearance and a superior affect. There was hardly enough room in the office for my family, the two doctors, and their extremely overblown egos.

This doctor began to rattle off in a bored monotone a list of things we could look forward to, the other doctor yawning. His description of the lives we were headed for was the single most depressing thing I'd ever heard. Our life expectancy would be shortened. We should not have children. Our muscles were going to deteriorate one by one. Before long, we'd be incapacitated and in wheelchairs.

As the doctor delivered this account of a future in which all our hopes and dreams were effectively over, I struggled to process what was happening. I still had no understanding of what our MD diagnosis meant. Sure, I had experienced some odd symptoms and there was my persistent fatigue, but it couldn't be that bad, right? I still looked and felt relatively normal, after all. There was no way this laundry list of horrors applied to me.

There was nothing that had happened to me previously that I could now draw upon to make sense of what I was hearing. I'd arrived at the clinic with my family thinking that this was going to be a routine appointment. That we'd be given some insights and suggestions, some sort of medication, and off we'd go. As I sat at that conference table, I was completely blindsided. I couldn't even begin to believe that the future the doctor was describing was a possibility.

What the doctors didn't expand on that day was anything remotely positive. Although they were supposed to be some of the top professionals in their field, they seemed to have missed out on the humanity part of their training. There we were, three out of four family members stricken with the same incurable, debilitating neuromuscular disease, and yet these doctors couldn't have been more callous or devastating if they had tried. Surely, they must have had some level of training on how to deliver this type of news in a remotely sensitive way? Because they hadn't talked to us during our "exams," the verdict the doctors now delivered was even more devastating. I was totally, utterly and completely stricken. As they laid out the grim prognosis, all I heard was "your life is over, you'll never amount to anything, you might as well end it now."

What was even worse was that even as they handed down this life-altering news, the doctors acted like this was just a routine conversation. They looked slightly bored, sneaking glances at their watches and yawning occasionally. I wanted to ask them what they were rushing through our meeting to get to. Clearly there was something much more important happening somewhere else.

At one point, Dr. Big Head mentioned that if we smoked, we should stop. "Well, your head is so far up your ass, you should try to take it out," was my response. I kept this to myself, along with all the other retorts that might have given the doctors an inkling of just how their words were affecting me. Did I mention that I can't stand being condescended to?

The irony was that the motto of this clinic was "providing help & hope." They pledged to "assist and empower families," and yet here we were, being treated like a slightly boring inconvenience. Instead of hope, we got the promise of a dismal half-life.

I can still remember that day in vivid detail. I can see the gleam of the conference table, hear the ticking of the clock on the wall, and feel my mother's fingers clawing into my leg as she tried to keep me from uttering my sarcastic comments. I can recall exactly what I was thinking as the meeting finally ended, the doctors gathering up their files and hurrying off to whatever more important engagement awaited them. "Who is going to want me now?"

SPITFIRE

In my life there have been several situations where I had a 50% chance of things going one way, or the other, basically either winning or losing. At birth, I had a 50% chance of survival and a 50% chance of inheriting a neuromuscular disorder. Since I survived the first couple days of my life, I obviously won that coin toss. With the inherited muscle disorder, I lost the coin toss.

Adversity is not something I am a stranger to. I have had many struggles in my life and many hurdles to overcome, starting from before I was born. I was born six weeks early in 1975, through a C-section as my mother was heading into kidney failure due to an extreme case of toxemia. She, too, was given a 50% chance of survival. I spent the first five weeks of my life in the Neonatal Intensive Care Unit (NICU). My father took some pictures of me, and when my mother saw them, she told him that he didn't know how to use a camera. I wasn't the cutest sight, being extremely tiny and resembling a plucked chicken. Even pictures taken several months later aren't all that attractive.

The NICU at the University of Vermont (UVM) medical center was started in the 1960s and was the only facility of its kind in the state of Vermont. The doctors in the NICU worked closely with those at Dartmouth Hitchcock hospital in New Hampshire, both of which are Level I trauma hospitals. Even though the NICU had been developed several years before my birth, had I been born a few years earlier I would have had a much lower chance of survival. One of the main issues that I faced was respiratory distress. Every day my blood gasses were taken to determine my oxygen saturation. The doctors at these two hospitals would discuss the results in order to determine the best course of action for that day.

I didn't see my mother for the five weeks that I was in the NICU. After being so sick herself, she was on bed rest once released from the hospital. My mother did come up to Burlington (an hour away) to see me once. However, it was so exhausting for her she couldn't do it again.

Spitfire

My parents' neighbor in New Haven, the husband of my godmother, would bring up breast milk from my mother in a cooler every morning. My mother believed, very strongly, in the importance and positive aspects of breast milk, as well as breastfeeding. We still have the sign that was taped to the cooler, identifying that it was mine. There is a picture of a car driving from "Smith Dairy" aptly named after our surname and ending at the Medical Center Hospital of Vermont (MCHV).

I was born with hyaline membrane disease, meaning that my lungs wouldn't stay inflated on their own and I was placed in an incubator. My father came up to visit me in the NICU, every day that he was able. The nurses in the NICU encouraged my father to touch me. He would put his hand in the incubator, and it would cover my entire body. He would take me out of the incubator and hold me and even give me a bottle, but in a very short amount of time I would begin turning blue due to lack of oxygen. My grandmother, who had nine children, would have her face pressed against the window of the NICU, dying to get her hands on me.

The NICU nurses had given me the nickname of "spitfire." My parents assumed this was mainly for their benefit since my situation was precarious at best, and this would give them some encouragement. For most people, the word spitfire recalls an airplane used in WWII or perhaps someone with a fiery personality who is quick to anger and highly emotional. However, to my parents and me, it has a very different meaning. To us a spitfire is strong, defies the odds, and is tough. Although it seems somewhat ludicrous to call a scrawny, 3.2lb baby strong or tough, this is nonetheless who and what I am.

I wasn't allowed to leave the hospital until I reached the robust weight of four pounds. My mother was very nervous about me coming home and was worried about being able to take care of me since she was still recovering from being very ill herself. When she learned that the nurses were giving me formula, in addition to breast milk, my mother decided she could take better care of me than that. Another condition for my release, being that I was born in October, was my parents installing baseboard heat in their house that previously only had a wood stove for heat. (My mother claims I was a pain in the ass from the very beginning.)

Recently, my mother and I reviewed the records from the hospital and mementos from my first few weeks at home. My parents had only been able to afford catastrophic health insurance with a $10,000 deductible. The bills for my mother and me ran to 15 pages. The final amount came to just under the deductible. There were feeding charts recording every time I ate, and how much. Once I was home, I had to be nursed every few hours because it would exhaust me to the point that I would fall asleep before getting enough calories. There were two medical records for three and four months after I was born recording my weight, length, and head circumference. There was also a letter my mother had written to her sister that talked about getting together in the spring, when I would be able to go outside.

The nickname "spitfire" has really shown who I have been in dealing with the struggles in my life. I often have wanted to give up, throw in the towel, and end any form of suffering. But I don't. I keep going every day; even when small tasks seem insurmountable. No matter what is in front of me, my determination gets me through. It causes me to continue putting one foot in front of the other, one step at a time. In the end, all I can do is persevere. I am a spitfire, in the most positive sense of the word.

To this day, I have scars on both my wrist and ankle from IVs and blood being drawn. They are small and faint, but noticeable. I remember, as a young child, questioning my mother about how I had gotten them and where they were from. I don't remember her response, but I learned early on what a struggle the first few days of my life had been. These scars are medals of honor, or bravery, and they signify the will I have had since the very first hours and days of my life.

MY ELEMENT
2018

As I arrived at the courts, I took a deep breath and smiled. I was back in my element, and I couldn't wait for my first match to begin. I registered, got my court assignment, and acclimatized to the conditions. Greeting friends, I settled in to watch the matches in progress until it was my turn to take the court. Even before I got out there, I was mentally preparing myself for the match ahead. I visualized my movement on the court and thought about my shot selection. I did a little physical warm-up, rolling around until the wheelchair feels like an extension of me. When it was almost time, I taped the racket to my hand and followed the various steps that now felt like second nature to me. And then I rolled out onto the court.

The sun was warm on my head, and I could feel the nerves running through my body as I took some practice swings with my racket and waited to hit a return shot. We were just getting warm, but I felt my body start heating up. This was the place and time I loved: the beginning of a match, where I am doing something I'm good at, in a place where I belong. I was seen here as an athlete and a competitor. I smiled, glad to be back.

The rhythm of the match feels like home to me. I serve and return, my opponent and I switching court ends on odd-numbered games. The thwack of balls being hit, the grunts that accompany a good smash of the ball, the exhalation that follows a serve, the applause of the crowd — this is my soundtrack. I even love the smells of tennis: the distinctive aroma of courts baking in the sun, the tang of new tennis balls, the slightly antiseptic scent of athletic tape. Even my own sweat smells good to me when I'm out here in my element.

While I love to win and will compete ferociously to try to get there, winning isn't the main goal. The most important thing is that I'm out on the court, being completely engaged in an activity I love. While winning is, of course, preferable to losing, my focus is on the elements of the game. I'm continually moving, trying to hit the ball well-deep, angled shots that will be hard for my opponent to return, then predicting where her shots will go. I'm focused on serving consistently and repositioning after every single shot I hit.

When I first started playing wheelchair tennis, I had a constant desire to get out of my chair. I felt so awkward and uncoordinated in the chair. It weighed me down and encumbered me. I longed to be able to say, "enough of this" and to stand up, exerting my domination of the court, my opponent and the match, just as I'd done so often in the days before I got sick.

I never feel that impulse anymore. All the things that I so longed for in my early days as a wheelchair athlete are within reach now. As my skills have improved, my sense of myself as an athlete has returned. That piece of myself that I'd feared was lost for good is back. I haven't been reborn, but I have regained my life and myself. I am once again a spitfire. A spitfire on wheels.

PART TWO

GRIP

GRIP

The sun streamed in through the kitchen windows, glinting off the snow that was piled up outside. I was eight years old and looking forward to oatmeal for breakfast and a snow-day off from school. I climbed up onto a stool at the kitchen table. There was something I wanted to show my mom.

"Look!" I instructed her, holding out my fist. I'd pulled my fingers in as tightly as I could, but now, when I tried to open my hand, nothing happened. My mother looked puzzled, then startled.

"You try," I said, sliding my fist toward her so that she could pry my fingers into the correct position. She still couldn't get them to release without pulling very strenuously. I howled in protest. My fingers were locked into the closed position, and I had to use all the muscles in my hand to finally get them to release.

If my mother was concerned, she didn't let on. She seemed to think that having a fist that didn't want to let go was a sign of my unique individuality. I wasn't that worried, either. My hand was a source of curiosity to me. Before long, I'd forgotten all about it.

Several years later, I was at field hockey practice. A physical therapist had come to evaluate us, and one of the tests involved grip strength. She gave us an instrument to hold and instructed us to squeeze as hard as we could. The first part of the test was easy for me. At this point in my life, I had no trouble gripping the hell out of anything. When she signaled for me to open my hand, I couldn't do it.

"The test is over," she said, her tone annoyed. "You can let go now."

But my fingers wouldn't release. As I struggled to open my fist, the PT finally pulled the instrument out of my hand. She probably thought I was just trying to be funny.

My grip strength—specifically the lack of it—was an issue that appeared periodically. I would think about it for a minute, shrug, and go on my way. As a kid, I loved nothing more than swinging from the monkey bars at the playground. As I got older, I realized that my hands now tended to slip. The same thing happened in college when I tried to hang from a zipline. Our neighbors in Vermont had one of these in their yard when I was growing up, and I'd loved the feeling of sailing through the air. Now when I tried it, I couldn't hang onto the bar.

My inability to reopen my hand after I'd made a fist or clenched my fingers also got harder to ignore. During the summer I was eighteen, I broke several of my fingers by putting them through the wire mesh door at the tennis court. Everybody would put their fingers through the mesh since it was the easiest way to open the gate. The problem was that my fingers didn't seem to want to let go. As I started to walk around the open gate, my fingers would still be gripping the wire. After they held on to the point of breaking, I stopped doing this.

Get a grip, I often tell myself. The spirit of this phrase is right there on my to-do lists and in my planner: get organized. Get your shit together. The "grip" that I'm forever after means holding onto things, following through, and not giving up. I blame my tendency to let things slide or get away from me on my lack of grip strength. My extreme fatigue means that I fight, almost every day, the urge to give in and let go. The feeling is like clinging to the edge of a cliff, digging in with my fingernails, trying my best to avoid tumbling into the abyss. Get a grip.

When I was a kid, I had a firm grip on life. I knew who I was and what I wanted. As I became a teenager, my grip started to slip, even as my actual physical grip was now a tight fist that wouldn't unclench. My prowess in sports, especially in tennis, was still a strong part of my identity. No matter what else was happening around me, I was a damned good athlete. I was losing a sense of who I was.

When I went to boarding school, I really started to lose my grip. More and more symptoms of my as-yet-undiagnosed disability were appearing. While I was still an amazing athlete and could perform well, it was taking more and more effort. My exertions on the court or the playing field left me increasingly exhausted. I'd never liked running, except for sprinting during a match or game or Indian sprints in a

Grip

warm-up, but now I began to really struggle. I could barely finish the mandatory run before field hockey practice. The will was still there, but my abilities were declining rapidly, my body beginning to fail me.

Lost in the fog of adolescence and away from home at a school that was difficult for me, I could feel my grip slipping. I'd been holding on to my identity as an athlete, the thing that was the most valuable to me. Now that was slipping away like a greased, fraying rope through my fingers. I had almost no strength to pull myself back up.

When I left Vermont and headed out to California to start college, I vowed things would be different this time. I gripped onto the idea that I could leave the pain, struggles, and disillusionments behind. In many ways, it worked. The struggles and the symptoms were still there, but I found friends who helped me again and again when my grip threatened to slip. When I almost didn't graduate because the demons I was battling had a stronger grip on me than I had on myself, my friends were there. Thanks to them I got my grip back, though it would never be as strong as it had been initially.

Even as I regained one kind of grip, the other was flagging. There was no denying now that my hands and fingers were gradually weakening. I thought of it as being like a game of tug of war that I was slowly losing. In childhood, there was little to no weight at the other end of the rope, meaning that I barely had to do anything. As I got older, I needed to exert more effort and to continually tighten my grip just to hold on. Even as I worked harder, it was getting more and more difficult to maintain a firm grip on my end of the rope.

Getting diagnosed at age 25 would finally explain the mystery behind my clenched fingers, my sliding palms. If anything it made hanging on even harder. I needed a firm grip on my reality and my sanity just to keep it together. These days I often struggle to open bottles, unlock doors, or use keys, but I can hold onto what I have, enough to make my life work. Then there are the times when my grip slips. That's when I realize just how tenuous is my hold on all the things and people around me, the people that I most need to cling to. That's when I hang on for dear life.

ATHLETE AT HEART

As a small child I learned how to skate on double runner skates, pushing a chair in front of me for balance. I began to take part in the Middlebury College winter carnival ice show. Then skating became my passion.

Starting in fourth grade I took lessons at Leddy Park in Burlington during the week, and I skated on the weekends and before school at the college rink. From all my other activities I had legs that were extremely strong, and I was fearless. I had huge jumps, incredible speed, and I loved to skate. I loved the exhilarating feeling of the strength in my legs and arms, the wind produced from my speed blowing my hair back, the incredible feeling of excelling at an activity, and the way my body and muscles would feel after a hard workout.

At that time, I didn't feel tired, I just felt good. Anything I asked my body to do while I was on the ice it did. While I had professional lessons and attended skating camp in the summer, I would skate and practice on my own as well. One of the advantages of my mom being on the athletic staff at the college was that she had keys to the ice rink.

I competed in several competitions in Burlington and twice at the Olympic Rink in Lake Placid, New York. Because of all the other activities I did, including many weekends spent traveling to out-of-town ski races, there wasn't much time for skating competitions.

For years I had solos in the ice show, and it was so invigorating. There are many stories about my poise during my ice show solos. One year, the fire alarm went off right in the middle of my performance and I couldn't hear the music for my program. I kept skating, however, and completed my program perfectly.

Another year my teacher had to add extra music because I could never complete the program without falling. In the performance, I got to add extra things to do at the end because when I was in the spotlight, I didn't fall. For years I had been working on my axel jump, one and a half revolutions. I had never landed on one foot, although I went about three feet in the air and traveled almost six. People were amazed by my skill, my persistence, and my ability to rise to the occasion. When it came time to do the axel during my program, I landed it perfectly.

I wanted to go to the Olympics. One of the things I prided myself on was my sit spin. I could go all the way down into a sit, and all the way up, without having to push off my knee like most others did. The ice show was a Saturday night and a Sunday matinee, and in my last performance on Sunday, the year I was 16 and in my last ice show, I had to push on my knee to come back up. What I didn't realize at the time was that I was experiencing my first symptoms of MMD and no longer had the reserves I needed to show two days in a row. I had given it my all the night before. Puzzling, but since I had no idea of what was to come, I brushed it off.

However, I decided to attend boarding school in Connecticut starting my junior year and skated less and less. The last ice show I was in was my sophomore year in high school.

There were many things like this, when I look back through my childhood and adolescence, that were harbingers of this disease that I just ignored and only remembered when I received my diagnosis.

Throughout my childhood and adolescence, I did many different sports. I played field hockey starting in the fourth grade until halfway through my senior year of high school. I started playing on the school team in junior high and continued through high school. Although field hockey wasn't a sport I was crazy about, the fact that I was an amazing athlete made me sufficient at any sport. Sophomore year of high school I was the high scorer.

During my junior year of high school, at boarding school, I got the winning goal in the game and a large headline in the newspaper. Although this didn't make me any more popular at school or on the team, I enjoyed the slight celebrity status that it gave me among some of my peers.

I quit field hockey during my senior year of high school, which was something I had threatened for several years but never done. I had begun to loathe the struggle I had developed with the long-distance runs at the beginning of practice. Running has always been a difficult thing for me, in terms of long-distance—I have always been a fast and kickass sprinter—and I knew halfway through the seasons the runs would double and I just wasn't up to it. Again, I was experiencing early symptoms of MMD.

When I went to see my coach to tell her I was quitting the team she asked to come to one more practice and give it 100 percent. Although I liked to think I was always giving 100 percent, apparently, I wasn't. I met with her after the practice, and she said if I always practiced like that, I would be a starter in every game. However, I was barely able to make it back to my dorm from the field. Subconsciously, my body had known that I needed to conserve a little energy and wasn't letting me give everything I had. I quit the very next day.

I started playing tennis when I was eight or nine and ended up being an All-American my freshman year in college, after which I stopped playing competitively (or as uncompetitive as a competitive person can). During the summer when I was growing up, I played in a tennis league where we competed every week with different country clubs. We had team practice once a week and on Fridays would travel or have other teams come to us. I enjoyed the competitions and going to the very fancy clubs in the area. I competed in tournaments throughout the year, both in Vermont and traveling to other states. I played in different tournaments that were held at my tennis club and I also competed in junior tournaments.

Throughout my four tennis seasons in high school, out of hundreds of matches, I lost a total of eight. This is an unbelievable record. I remember with clarity the eight matches that I lost. I was undefeated every season except for two matches, and it was phenomenal.

I played in invitational tournaments with my mother, who was the associate athletic director and tennis coach at Middlebury College. We would play both as mixed doubles and singles matches. I played against opponents who were better, and I always rose to the occasion. The only person who beat me with any regularity was my mother. While in competition against each other, during member guest or mixed doubles matches all the spectators (except for my father who claimed to be supporting us both) cheered for me. It was fun to root for the underdog, as my mother tended to win at every athletic competition she engaged in. The crowd was ready for someone else to win. Sometimes, I did.

Tennis became a major sport for me, and it was through tennis that I had one of my first experiences of winning and realizing how much I liked the rushing sensation of pride and recognition for putting in hard work. The more you excel at something the more you win and the more you win the more you like it and almost come to expect it.

For me, it was the competition even more than the winning that I enjoyed but again, I did win almost every time. Above all, I was a fierce competitor with determination and tenacity, and I never gave up, which made it possible for me to win matches against better opponents or matches I should have lost.

Through my late teens and early twenties, I was a tennis instructor in the summer. I gave private lessons, group lessons and ran the practices and matches I had once been a part of. It is a long and tiring day standing out in the sun on the hot courts, but I loved tennis.

I still love to play tennis with my mother to this day. Although half an hour is about my limit, it is still one of my favorite activities. I love to go and watch the tournaments my mother plays in. I watch all the grand slams on television, and one of my dreams is to attend the Australian Open.

I grew up sailing and attended a several-week summer sailing program for two or three summers. I don't remember being asked if I wanted to go to sailing camp, I just ended up there. I didn't really like sailing. I love being on or near the water, but sailing was never a passion for me the way it was for the rest of my family. There were many other activities that I liked much better. I was interested in too many other things to spend much time sailing.

I have been skiing since before I was six and spent most weekends in the winter skiing all day. I ski raced as a teenager and was on the ski team my freshman year in high school. I have many wonderful memories of skiing and ski vacations (although I always lobbied to go somewhere warm).

Athlete at Heart

When I was 10, I competed in skiing in the Junior Olympics. I didn't really understand that I was competing, but felt excited and I wanted to go through the gates. After the race they prepared for the award ceremony in the lodge while I was having lunch with my mother. While I was interested in the results, as soon as we were finished, he suggested we continue skiing, so I never knew who won.

Towards the end of the day, when we went back to the lodge to take off our boots, I realized that no one had received the silver medal. Curious, I went up to the official at the desk and asked who had won it, never dreaming it would be someone I knew. She told me that it was someone named Leslie Smith and I replied, "That's me!!!" The medal hanging around my neck seemed out of place in the picture of me that my mom took with my somewhat absurd-looking ski outfit.

Now, for the most part, our family has been more concerned about one's ability to do something rather than how one looks doing it, including having all the right equipment and fancy trappings. I never had the newest or best equipment or clothing until I was an extremely accomplished skier.

An example of this value is from when I was learning to ride a bike. My mother bought a bike at a yard sale for a dollar and told me that I couldn't get a new bike until I learned to ride the one that I had. I spent hours trying and trying to ride this bike with no success.

One day I was playing at a friend's house, and he had a new bike. When my mother came to pick me up, I showed her how well I could ride his bike. When we got home and she examined my yard sale bike more closely, she realized that it was broken and wasn't possible for anyone to ride. The next day my father bought me a brand-new blue Schwinn bicycle.

This lesson was replicated in my skiing gear as I am sure my skis were not only old but very unfashionable. I had a hat that was way too big, snow pants that I detested and were repaired with duct tape, and yet I had a big smile on my face. I may have looked somewhat silly and had begged my mom for ski pants so I didn't have to wear my dreaded overall snow pants, but I was a darn good skier.

Between the ages of 10 and 13, there was a ski team called Hopefuls that was divided by ages. I won several of the races and remember the headlines I got in the newspaper, such as "Leslie Smith led the pack of 12-year old's..." Throughout the years, I have had several newspaper headlines.

In the summers, I went to different camps for all the sports I did as well as regular camp. All my camps were focused on either a specific sport or were based in the outdoor wilderness with activities all day long. I didn't have a lot of downtime whether it was summer, winter, spring, or fall.

At age six, I started taking horseback lessons at the farm across the street from where I lived. There was a girl who lived there of my same age, and we became very good friends. I rode all the way through my adolescence and had my own pony. Since I lived in the country, we were able to have a pasture for my horse and go on rides through the fields. I still love horses.

With all these different sports, it was hard to focus on just one.

For several years my mom and I would meet to ski together at Mad River. This is the ski area with the slogan "Mad River Glen, Ski it If you can." I had grown up skiing there and loved it, the long trails, skiing the bumps and riding the only single chair around. The trails aren't groomed, and it is tough. However, I usually ski once or twice a season with my mom. The last time I went skiing in my late thirties, things had changed. I skied the first run, and I thought my legs were going to give out. Halfway down the trail, I sat down since my legs were screaming. The only difficulty after that was that I couldn't get up without a lot of effort and some assistance. I was used to skiing from top to bottom with only a short stop at mid-station. This was yet another new experience. I only ended up skiing two runs that day.

Over the next few years, this love of athletics was reinforced over and over. I love snowshoeing. In recent years we haven't had enough snow to do it with any regularity. When a friend came to visit a few winters ago, I was 35 years old. It was during a snowstorm, and we decided to go out in the park next to my house. We went for about an hour or the equivalent of about two miles, taking periodic rest stops and with her breaking trail. It was snowing and cold and wonderful. The feeling of exertion, my hair freezing from the snow, the fresh air, the enjoyment of the activity, it was positively the best feeling ever, albeit exhausting.

The next day, I literally could not get out of bed. It is like being slapped in the face when you realize that your body will just up and quit. Even though I was able to do the activity, I was no longer able to continue normal life activities after I was done.

It always amazes me that I forget this fact. I know that I have limitations and I know I need extensive recovery time; none of this is new information. When I couldn't get out of bed though I was totally dumbfounded. And I know, without a doubt, that I will forget again and again what and how significant my limitations are. In some ways, it is like looking in the mirror and still expecting to see a vision of a self I haven't seen in 10 years. It is not ignorance or denial or even forgetfulness or wishful thinking. I still consistently have a vision of myself that doesn't match up to the actual picture, or in this case doesn't match up to what the ability is.

When asking one of my lifelong friends, Kelly Hagman, whom I met while in college, about my disease progression, she stated: "Physically, since I see Leslie all the time, I feel that it is difficult to notice any of the subtle differences. We both still think we look 18. In a lot of ways, I feel there has only been minor progression, but when I look carefully, I can see that Leslie is not pushing herself like she would in the past. That's the major difference. We would go to do something, and Leslie would do it no matter what, or try, and be frustrated with herself if she got tired, but now I feel that she has very reasonable limits and reasonable expectations for herself and sets the day out with those expectations in mind. For me, that is the most pronounced difference I've seen over time."

I was and will continue to be an athlete. While simple athletic activities are about all I can do at this point, I can remember the way it felt to be incredible and invincible at any athletic activity. I still have the muscle memory of years of all sorts of different athletic feats. Although most of my genetic material didn't do so much for me, I did inherit the muscular build of my mother. This has kept me mobile and contributed greatly to the strength I have had my entire life.

Spitfire

My friend Kelly often laments the fact that she runs and does a lot more activity than I do, but I have more defined leg muscles than she does. I told her this was because from sunup until sundown as a child, I was moving; the faster, the better. One of my great joys was being better and faster than everyone, especially the boys. Anything that was put before me, I accomplished. That is still so important to me. While others see me as disabled and I may refer to myself as such, at heart, I am still the athlete I was.

APPLYING TO COLLEGE

In the fall of my senior year of high school I visited several colleges that were in New England and some others that were around the country, including in Virginia, Colorado, and California. I was interested in attending an all-women's college and decided to apply to around 10 different schools. Between my stellar high school tennis record and the fact that I had attended one of the top ten private schools in the country, I had some strengths as an applicant. I had little interest in attending some of the schools that I applied to, but I wanted a wide variety to choose from, including some longshots and some safeties.

I had applied early decision to Middlebury College, which initially was my first choice. Although I was accepted during general admission, I decided that staying in my hometown and playing tennis on the team my mom coached wasn't the best idea.

One of the reasons I didn't end up enrolling at any of the small liberal arts schools that I'd applied to in New England was my fear that any college I would choose had a high risk of just being a continuation of the issues I'd faced in high school including isolation and loneliness. I did not want to end up surrounded by the same people.

The summer before my senior year, I had attended a science camp at Hollins College in Virginia. Since it was a small, all-women's, Liberal Arts College and I had enjoyed the school and surrounding area when I had been there; I thought it would be a good fit. After getting off the waitlist at Scripps, a school I had applied to on a whim, it rose to the top of my list. Once I saw the campus, I was totally sold.

One of the deciding factors was tennis. I planned on playing on the college team. I spoke with a lot of school coaches and was recruited by several of them. When I visited Scripps College of the Claremont Colleges after graduation, I met with the tennis coach and became excited by the prospect of being part of her team and becoming an NCAA player.

Scripps was, and is, in a class of its own. It is covered with the most amazing vegetation and flowers, Mediterranean-style buildings with red-tiled roofs, wrought iron railings on porches, and everywhere you looked there were orange trees, fountains, beautiful lawns, and the sense of a whole new world. It had an incredible smell, and I could totally see myself there. When my parents took me to visit, I was enthralled. As a few days passed and I became accustomed to this alternate universe, I realized this was where I was meant to be. This could be what I was looking for. I had the highest expectations for the transformation that would occur as I stepped back on that campus as an enrolled student.

One thing was for sure, this was a different world, and after I visited the school, I couldn't wait to come. I was so tired of the east coast and New England and the same people I had known all my life and all the judgments, the freezing cold winters, and what I had come to feel was the absolute lack of anything fun, new, or interesting. I longed to get out of the awful situation I had experienced in high school and find new, open-minded people who hadn't known me my whole life. I was looking forward to exposure to new and different things.

All I knew was I needed to get the hell out of Dodge. Surely baggage couldn't follow me across the country. It took a while to catch up with me, but when it did it was with a vengeance. But I wasn't worried about that. All I needed to do was convince my parents, pack my bags, and hit the road. Eventually, I convinced them and was on my way.

Looking back at college and my ability to travel across the country on my own, not knowing anyone, I am amazed that I did it without a second thought. I remember many wonderful things. There were also many mysteries I experienced with my body's limitations that I would later come to understand were due to MMD.

INCIPIT VITA NOVA
"New life begins"
1994

In April of my senior year of high school I was sitting on a bench at the tennis courts watching my teammates' matches. I was with my dad, who had come for the weekend to watch me play.

"I have a surprise for you," he said, smiling at me.

"What is it?"

"I'll give you a hint. It's seven letters long."

Without hesitating, I knew the answer. "I got into Scripps?"

"That's right!"

When I had received the responses from the colleges I had applied to, I learned that I had been initially waitlisted at Scripps. Even though I had applied there on a whim, that day in April, it had rushed to the forefront of my mind as an answer to all my prayers.

My parents decided we would go out to California and visit Scripps a few days after my high school graduation. I would tour the campus, meet the tennis coach, and try to determine if it was the place for me.

When I look back at visiting Scripps when I was 18, the picture in my head is still so vivid. I can still smell the flowers that were everywhere and see the entire campus in complete detail. I remember trying to fit the image I had of myself into this world of stucco buildings with red tile roofs, hundreds of fountains and the most amazing birds of paradise flowers. In a completely altered universe would I be able to regain my sense of self?

I remember the emotions that I felt between my first visit until I graduated four years later. My expectation of sheer bliss with all my emotional struggles behind me was, of course, a bit too good to be true. I experienced many coming-of-age and emotional struggles as all young adults do. Despite the difficulties I faced, physically and emotionally, those were some of the best years of my life. I can feel the sun and warmth, see the snow-capped mountains in the distance, recall the layout of each of my and many of my friends' dorm rooms, and still hear the laughter that we shared.

I saw Scripps as the brass ring, the thing I was looking for to save my life, and give me a way out of all the struggles, depression, and sadness that had been plaguing me. Somehow, I knew that a "new life" would begin here, and I could change and have another chance at a life I wanted to be living.

Going to Scripps was a huge turning point in my life. I shudder to think where I would be, what I would be doing, and how different my life would be had I not gone there. Despite the baggage I arrived with, I was able to put it aside several times and rise to the occasion that outstripped my expectations and gave me back parts of myself that I hadn't known were missing but felt the emptiness that was left in their place just the same.

I had a visceral reaction to Scripps. Even though I was in some ways a fish out of water, I knew it was a pond I wanted to be swimming in. I showed up with overalls and Birkenstocks and ended up in a world of belly shirts and miniskirts. In many ways it was an easy adaptation. All the sights and smells, the little and big differences, became commonplace quickly, although they were quite startling at first. It was as though I was able to shed my skin of unhappiness and desolation and underneath was a new, clean, happy one. I was a phoenix rising from the ashes.

REGAINING GRIP

I had tried the tactic of leaving one place for a brand new one in hopes of leaving all my problems behind, and similarly, the results were less than stellar. I left my home and the public high school that served six surrounding towns and ventured to Connecticut to attend the Loomis Chaffee School. I couldn't wait to get out of Vermont and figured that this would be a wonderful and amazing opportunity, athletically and academically.

My brother had left for boarding school the previous year and it looked like a good decision. Besides, I would no longer be the only child under my parents' supervision, and I could escape from the same people that I had known my whole life. Also, it seemed like an adventure.

As I have many times in my life, I once again fell for the misguided notion that the devil you don't know is bound to be as good or better than the devil you know. I came to find out, as I had before, you should always stick with the devil you know, because the one you don't can be worse than the devil himself.

I couldn't understand why I had such a hard time in boarding school. I am quite a nice person and very friendly. I now have some idea that it was the culmination of significant facts that caused me problems. The fact that I had entered the school as a junior, when cliques were already formed, hadn't helped matters.

The fact that I made varsity field hockey and had a headline in the newspaper a few weeks after I got there also did not help with teenage jealousy. I was sought after by many of the popular guys, and the fact that I wasn't humble and shy also conspired against me. It did however teach me several lessons about human nature and the art of being superficial.

I had never encountered superficiality before, and I've never learned how to be superficial. I didn't offer that much information about myself so ridiculous rumors got started. Girls I had considered friends junior year dropped me over the summer when they realized they couldn't be popular if they were friends with me.

Being myself was apparently not a route that would bring about good results. My self-esteem, which was already low, dropped out the bottom, but I did the best I could to persevere.

A girl in my junior year class said that it wasn't where we were that was making us so miserable, it was just the time in our lives. I think to some extent this is true, as adolescence is not a period I would return to for any reason. Loomis was without a doubt a poor choice for me and I was justifiably miserable.

I called home in tears most nights but didn't want to return to VT and public school. I have not been as unhappy, before or since, despite all the unpleasantness the future would hold for me. By the time I graduated from high school any self-esteem I had, or belief in myself, was destroyed.

It took me several years to be able to see the positives I gained from going to Loomis. I will be thankful for the opportunity to go to a college I otherwise would not have been accepted by, and it made it possible for me to be successful once there.

Coming off the two worst, depressing, and miserable years of my life at boarding school I made one firm decision. I was going to be myself at college no matter what, and my classmates could take me or leave me. To my great surprise and delight they took me.

GRIP WITH BOTH HANDS

I loved everything about Scripps from the moment I got there, except for my roommates. I couldn't imagine people who could be less like me and, at first, I had the sickening feeling that I had made a huge mistake. I was the third roommate in a double that had become a triple room. It quickly became clear to me that we were going to need bunk beds. This first girl who had arrived had already selected a bed, a dresser and a desk and didn't make a great first impression. I had previously talked on the phone to the third roommate who hadn't made a much better impression and I could see my fear of being a fish out of water like I'd been at Loomis approaching.

People stopped by to see how we were organizing our room. There were many others in the same boat of having a double room transformed into a triple. I could see this wasn't turning into the dream I'd been having about awesome roommates and tons of new friends. I couldn't have met two people who were less like me and now I was expected to live with them?

Luckily, at my peer mentor group that evening I met several other women who I knew would become my close friends. The fear I had that this had been a bad choice and I was going to be as uncomfortable and unable to fit in as I had been in high school began to fade.

As orientation began and I met the other girls in my dorm things started to come together for me. On one of the activities, a trip to Venice beach, a girl from my dorm and I went rollerblading together, and later that night many of us got ready together for the first party of the school year. As I looked around the large group of women who had become my friends, I realized that this was the best decision I had made so far. I knew that my new life had begun.

Once classes began and positive changes continued one after the other, I began to shake off the low opinion I had of myself, and my bold and friendly personality started to emerge again.

The first spring I was at Scripps College I played on the varsity tennis team. I ended the semester on academic probation and my friends all complained that I was either at tennis, class, or sleeping. It was considered that there were three aspects of college: academics, sports, and social life. It was next to impossible to do all three. Part of my struggle was that I wanted to participate in all three and some area had to take the hit.

Essentially, all three of the areas were negatively impacted. It got worse over the next three years. My friend Kelly took a picture of me in bed and said she could use it to remember my senior year. I was always tired and, left to my own devices, would sleep over 12 hours. I couldn't understand why I was tired all the time.

As usual, when my body won't do something I want it to, I blame myself and figure I am just a lame loser. Self-flagellation doesn't make anything better, but anger is a place that I can reach quite quickly when I feel like I am failing myself.

By the end of senior year, I was barely passing my classes and wasn't even living in the dorms. I was clinging by my fingernails and felt like the bright future I'd planned on had gone up in flames in front of me and all that was left was smoldering ashes with no rising phoenix in sight. My world was black and white and mostly gray, and I didn't see any way to get out of this alive. I was almost completely unable to graduate, in a state of suicidal depression, and never thought I would be happy again.

Thankfully, I was wrong. But I had no idea of what was to come.

STRENGTHENING GRIP

In the spring of 2002, at age 26, I realized my current life circumstances needed to change. It had been over a year and a half since my diagnosis and I had withstood the shock and waited for the dust to settle, but I had never taken the time to examine or even begin to come to terms with what this diagnosis meant for me.

I was planning on applying to graduate schools in the fall for the class of 2003 and my mother suggested I talk to her advisor at University of Vermont (UVM) to see if she could assist me with the application process in hopes of making my application stronger. While in conversation with this woman she told me that they had rolling applications that year for the MSW program. She took me over to the social work department and I made an appointment for that afternoon.

When I returned later in the day, I met with several members of the social work department. I had known since I had applied previously and not gotten in, that if they had a chance to talk to me, I had a much better shot at getting accepted. I have always been able to talk a good game and could back it up. I came away from this meeting having made a favorable impression and began the application process.

I felt a need to regroup and recharge before hopefully starting on my next step of grad school. In the previous two years, I had just been receiving information about the diagnosis but had not been able to take it in, and I needed to develop a different lens to view my life and future through rather than the one I had been using my whole life. It was clear that I needed a chance to stop and breathe.

To this end, I decided to take a medical leave of absence from my job the summer of 2002, come to terms with my diagnosis, and find a way to move forward. My mother supported my plan to have a healing summer; in fact, she was the one who suggested it. After being granted a medical leave from work I began to plan.

I was starting off with a Wellness Week at a meditation center in New York. That would be followed by a two week trip to California to visit various friends and attend a Scripps College summer event for alumnae called "Camp Scripps." I had a stack of inspirational books to use as guides for a different view and I was ready to embark on my summer of self-discovery.

I needed to learn to accept myself and the diagnosis I had been given. I spent a lot of time at the beach and had time to reflect and find a new perspective. I was on a personal journey to find peace, accept my new life and assimilate into a life that I wanted to live. I had heard and/or found the restrictions that would be part of my life and now I needed to find the flip side of the limitations. If certain avenues were now closed to me what new, healthy, and acceptable avenues would become open to take their place?

I realized I wouldn't find all the answers and my life wouldn't be healed in one summer, but it was a place to start. It was a brief respite from all the distractions in my life that were making it difficult for me to attend to myself. This was a chance to begin to find a way to come into grace and find peace...if even only for a moment in time.

PART THREE

LOVE

LOVE

Love is one of my favorite words. The first thing you will see when you walk into my house is a big sign on my wall that says "love." There are very few places in my house where you don't see the word love several times. I even have "love" tattooed on my wrist.

Similarly, to my very strong relationship with the word "love," I also am very fond of hearts, which are the universal sign for love. Seeing hearts or the word "love" makes me smile and feel happy.

Amongst these expressions of love, I have several other pictures and decorations that depict things in my life that are important to me. Pictures of elephants, beach scenes, angels, signs saying things such as "hope," or "joy," or one of my personal favorites, "May you always have a shell in your pocket and sand in your shoes." All these decorations remind me to find love in the world around me as well as to feel hopeful and joyful in any way possible.

There are many different types of love: filial love, platonic love, romantic love, and unrequited love. We are constantly using "love" to describe something we may just like. Love can be used as a descriptive word and can lose a lot of strength by being overused or used in the place of "like" or "affection." I tell all those I love that I love them frequently. My husband and I say "I love you" to each other several times a day and we call each other "love." Although I use the word "love" frequently, I do not use it indiscriminately. If I use this word, I mean it.

Love can mean a variety of things. Need is often equated with love. When you need someone, the desire and necessity of being with them can be construed as love, or, in essence, you love them because you need them. The other side of this is you need them because you love them.

Love of and for yourself is one of the most important and often lacking types of love. In order to love another fully, you must first love yourself, which is one of the hardest kinds of love to gain and express. It may be that in order to love yourself, you also need to be able to accept yourself, wherever you may be now.

For me, this has been the most challenging love of all. Years of self-doubt, low or nonexistent self-esteem, absence of self-respect, and anger turned inward made it almost impossible for me to not only accept myself but to love myself as well.

I have my disability as a result of a loving relationship. I inherited it from my father, who had the same disability, although to a much lesser degree. My brother also inherited it. My father, by loving my mother and deciding to have children, unwittingly passed on the altered gene that has had a major and often brutal impact on our lives. The sting of it is somewhat lessened because of the deep, unconditional love that he gave us.

Unconditional love is perhaps the hardest love to find. The love that no matter who you are or what you do this love will never be rescinded. Most love, no matter how strong, is usually conditional.

All relationships go through changes and stages. In the beginning, when you are falling in love, everything seems so pure and perfect. Often, it is when real life begins to intrude that all the flaws you overlooked at the start become apparent and this is the stage where many relationships end.

If you make it past this point and can keep moving forward together, and make a life, you will continue onto the next stage and the next and the next. One of the many pitfalls is one partner moving through these stages faster or slower than the other, hence the phrase: "we grew apart."

There is sometimes the wistful nostalgia and longing for the excitement and simplicity of the first days, but hopefully something much stronger and much more real has emerged instead. We are so hesitant to leave the magic circle, within which you and the one whom you have fallen in love with exist. Love is complicated and messy, but it is one of the best feelings in the world.

MARRIAGE

2006 to present

I have a loving husband, without whom I would have been lost during my most difficult times. My husband and I had a connection that I had not shared with anyone before. We had a relationship that sustained us and gave us strength. It is hard to lose that first luster of a relationship that blocks out everything but the two of you, but we managed to feel like we were on our first date for several months. Eventually, we faced the burden of everyday distractions and entanglements that are part of every life.

Four months into the beginning of our relationship, while we were still in the first stages of getting to know each other, I became quite ill and needed to leave the home where we were living in Colorado to return to my hometown of Vermont. We knew we each had found the person with whom we were meant to spend our lives.

Eight months later, Rob was able to join me in Vermont and we continued our life together. Two years after he came east, we were married. The love and the connection that we celebrated that day continued to grow and evolve into an extremely strong bond, based on mutual respect, communication, and deep love.

When I began dating Rob, I was not interested in entering a relationship. I had just ended a four-year, tumultuous relationship and I needed time to focus on myself and get my bearings. I had finally concluded that being alone was better than being in a negative relationship. My last relationship felt like my last chance, and since I couldn't make that work, I no longer trusted my own judgment concerning relationships. This was just another example of a round peg, square hole, and an unfortunate pattern in my life. My ego was bruised, and I didn't feel that I was ready (or ever would be in the foreseeable future) to embark on a new relationship. Luckily, I somehow convinced myself to take one more chance.

When Rob asked me out, I said yes with some trepidation. Had anyone other than Rob asked me out I would have said no. The only reason I said yes was I had seen how caring and compassionate he was. When dealing with the death of a co-worker, I asked if he wanted a hug and neither one of us wanted to let go, and we held each other for several minutes. The embrace I shared with Rob let me know, more than words ever could, that he felt the way I did.

For several years I felt like our first date had never ended. It was one of the most amazing nights in my life and I was reminded again just how much had been missing in my previous relationships. I believe that Rob and I fell in love with each other that first night.

I told Rob that I had MMD, what that was, and gave a short explanation about it. He seemed unimpressed and I took his calm reaction to mean that he didn't really understand what I was saying and the severity of my condition. On our next few dates, I continued trying to explain it to him.

"I'm not sure you understand how this disease currently affects me and will continue affecting me."

"Are you trying to talk me out of having a relationship with you?"

"Absolutely not. I just want to make sure you have a clear understanding of what you are getting into. I've told you that I have pervasive fatigue, but I'm not sure you realize that means I'm tired ALL THE TIME. I have a pacemaker to keep my heart from beating too slowly and I probably will have further cardiac events. I can't do a lot of the physical activities you like to do, although I can still do some. Eventually, my mobility will be affected, and I probably will end up in a wheelchair."

"We can face that when and if it happens."

Finally, I relaxed about it and figured I had given him the information and if he wasn't worried about it then I wouldn't worry about it either. We had no idea of how the symptoms would progress and what each new day would bring in terms of my physical digression. Another reason for my apprehension was that a former boyfriend had told me that for anyone to be with me they had to give up a lot. A remark like that tends to stay with you and I didn't want anyone to have to sacrifice to be with me. Of course, this boyfriend often made

Marriage

me feel that he was doing me a big favor by being with me and he acted like being my boyfriend was taking one for the team!

Rob and I became completely inseparable. He dropped me off at work in the mornings and I picked him up in the evenings. We were totally entwined with each other. Despite my decision that I was done with relationships, I had fallen completely in love and knew I had finally found a keeper. My fear from the diagnosis that no one would ever want me faded.

I found something with Rob that I thought I would never find: Respect. I had seen my parent's relationships and the relationships of their friends, and it is obvious that respect is a key ingredient. I never gave a thought to the fact that respect was totally absent for the most part in the relationships I had been involved in thus far. In some, a vestige of respect was apparent and in others there was none to speak of.

When I look at my relationship with Rob, I know part of the reason we don't judge each other is because we aren't judgmental people. In our case it also has to do with the deep respect we feel for each other that keeps us from the negative actions that have been so often part of my romantic relationships. I knew communication, trust, honesty, and love were needed to make a relationship work and I know as well as anyone that love isn't enough. I never realized respect was one of the most important ingredients of all.

When my mother asked me what I loved about Rob, I told her that the first thing that I had noticed was that I felt so, so, safe with Rob. My boyfriends usually gave me the impression that if the going got tough, they would tell me to peace out and hit the road running, leaving me to face whatever was coming. With Rob, I had no doubt that he would put himself between any danger and me, no questions asked and no doubt about it. In hindsight, I realize that I also felt emotionally safe with Rob. That was a new situation for sure. My mother scoffed at my response to what I loved about Rob, but I knew what a rare man I had found. She seemed to think that safety or loyalty wasn't a valid reason to love someone or was something that would ever be in question with anyone I chose to be with.

There is a quote I have always loved from *"Celebration,"* by Mari Evens. "I will bring you a whole person and you will bring me a whole person and we will have us twice as much of love and everything..." (Evens, XI). Rob and I strived to be "whole people" and bring together the best of ourselves that we have to offer. The amazing thing about marriage is that you can bring all of yourselves, the good, the bad, the ugly; the combination of the worst and the best of yourself is what makes you whole.

It is such a relief to be able to be myself with Rob. To not have to exert the energy to be anything or anyone other than who I am. To be accepted as myself and loved for who that person is, rather than be seen only as who I am not or for what is determined to be lacking. To be seen as someone who is wonderful the way I am, and to be cherished for all my quirks and idiosyncrasies. Rob loves me so much, no matter what, whether I am happy and healthy or depressed and angry, and often more than I love myself. Even more than that he accepts me every minute of every day and meets me where I am. I am so accepting of everyone else, but less so of myself.

Our relationship changes and goes through different stages due to my neuromuscular condition, the normal course of life, and changes that occur in any relationship. As more time passed instead of continuing to grow together, we began to grow apart. The things that we had in common seemed to be less and less apparent, and the closeness and communication, the parts of our relationship I prided myself on, began to diminish as we drifted in different directions.

A rift started opening between us that neither of us wanted to acknowledge or address but we both could see. I had previously questioned whether our relationship would survive. I was unable or unwilling to have a conversation about this and Rob is very good at diverting my attention and not having any conversations he doesn't want to have. Over the last two years I had tried in every way I could think of to bring us back together and regain the closeness and intimacy that seems to be lacking, with little or no success.

A metaphor that came to me is as though Rob is a cookie. I can see the cookie and I would really like to eat it, but I can only get crumbs. These crumbs are not enough to sustain me and although I know how good the cookie would taste I am not sure how badly I really want it. Having a conversation about this was so hard, and because I love Rob so much and desperately didn't want to hurt him, I resisted having a conversation about it. I do know how amazing our relationship was and can be, but I knew things needed to change, although I don't know what those changes would be, or how to make them come about.

When it became glaringly clear to me that I could no longer put off the conversation I was shocked to realize that Rob was feeling the same way. In some ways, as we begin to unravel our marriage, our communication drastically improved, and the resentment that was building between us dissipated. Although it is sad when any relationship doesn't work, it is so beneficial if you are able to end it before you have destroyed each other.

We are both happier and can address the things we want to do in our lives as individuals that we weren't able to do as a couple. There is such a relief that we were able to end our marriage amicably and will continue to be part of each other's lives. Our love, acceptance, and respect for each other is still intact and for that I am thankful.

40-LOVE / LOVE-40

In tennis, love means the absence of a score. When the match starts both players are at love. This is a completely even score where all players are at the same place, with no advantages or disadvantages: an even playing field. There is an absence of any burdens, the need to come from behind, the poorly hit shot that caused you to lose the last game, the serve that you couldn't return. As in relationships, the beginning is pure and simple before all the other complications of life encroach. Once the first point is played the other elements of a tennis match begin to emerge.

I know the feeling well at the outset of a match. It's excitement, nerves, and the anticipation for your performance and the eventual outcome. You can feel the temperature, the breeze ruffling your hair, or the absence of a breath of wind. You can smell the scent that new balls have, the smell of the asphalt court baking in the sun and hear the sound of the rubber of tennis sneakers against the ground. You can feel your heartbeat accelerating as you prepare to serve or return. Once the first ball is hit these feelings diminish and your attention shifts as the match progresses. I enjoy the feeling and the senses that are activated at the beginning of a competition, after the coin toss, the warmup, in essence, the point of no return.

During each game, if you have 40-love there is a very good chance you will win the game, and vice versa, if you have love-40, you are at quite a deficit and are in danger of losing the game.

For the first part of my life, I was often at the 40-love score; I won at most of the areas of my life, with little disappointment or inability. I won most everything I tried, and if I didn't win, I usually came close. As my life progressed, starting at adolescence, this started to change and continued changing. I have ended up with the score generally being love-40 and I seemed to be losing, not only at many of the things and parts of my life that I loved, but also areas of my life that I took for granted or that had previously been easy for me.

Now in most games, I win one or two points, and even if I manage to be ahead, I can't seem to hold my lead long enough to win. At the last tournament I attended when I was 44 years old, I did everything I could to be as prepared as possible. I run the risk of trying to be prepared, thus tiring myself out, leaving me in a bigger deficit than if I hadn't trained at all. Luckily, that wasn't the case this time. It was a beautiful day. My husband had accompanied me to a tournament in Salem, Oregon, and I was excited to share this with him.

In my first-round match, I won the first set easily with a score of 6-0. My opponent didn't play poorly; I just played better. In the second set I was up 4-2, and although it was getting more and more competitive, I was feeling that I had a good chance to win.

Unfortunately, at this point, my opponent's game improved, and my desire and determination were completely smothered by the fact that I had no energy left. Since I lack any reserves, I just couldn't keep going. I did keep going but had little success. I lost the second set and then the third set tiebreaker. From a sure win, I had been defeated. It is so frustrating to have your level of play drop no matter how hard you try. In so many ways, this is a metaphor for life with MMD. By the second set my ability to continue at the same level is gone and I am unable to win on sheer grit alone.

The same situation occurred at a doubles match in Baton Rouge. My friend Michaela and I were playing in the men's C doubles draw. (Since there are a lot more men than women wheelchair players, it is often necessary to enter a men's draw because there aren't enough women for their own draw.)

We had won our first match easily and were in the second round. Earlier in the day, I had played an extremely tough three-hour singles match. When I came off the court and found out I had to play my doubles match, I burst into tears. I was embarrassed but was so exhausted that I couldn't help it. The officials conferred to see if we could postpone the match until the next day, but if we didn't play this match now, other competitors would have to play three matches the next day.

They asked me how much time I needed to recover, and I looked at them in desperation and asked how much time I had. I was thinking at least 12 hours but took the hour they gave me and tried my best to recover. I warned my doubles partner that she would need to carry most of the match, and to emphasize this, as I went to sit in my wheelchair, I completely missed, ending up on the metal foot plate. Now I was starting the match with a bruised and painful backside to add to my misery.

Despite all this, we won the first set and were ahead in the second. However, at about that time, Michaela triple-double-faulted, putting us at an extreme disadvantage, my tank was completely empty, and the match went rapidly downhill from there. These experiences, especially when my will is so strong, are so disappointing because I give everything I have and more and still come up short. In a very short time, we lost not only the second set but the third set tiebreaker as well. Unfortunately, this is a pattern that I know all too well.

To be on the losing end of tennis is called "love." We tend to think of love as only a positive thing, and we are continually searching for love, or trying to hold on to love, or letting something go because of love. Everyone learns at some point in their life that love, on its own, isn't enough to make a relationship work, but we are willing to give up a lot or overlook a lot of things because "being in love" feels so good. While in tennis, love means either nothing, losing, or loss, in most other aspects, it is seen as winning or a positive thing.

6-0, 6-0

When you win a match 6-0, 6-0, you have completely dominated and blown your competition out of the water. Your opponents were unable to win any game from you and even if they came close you have won every game in the match. Granted, the final score doesn't always demonstrate how close or challenging a match is.

Losing a match at this score is a clear sign that you have done something wrong. Maybe your opponent was too powerful, and you were totally off your game, but to not even get on the scoreboard leaves a very strong sting of defeat. The only way to get redemption is to get up, practice some more, and work to do better the next time. Sometimes this isn't entirely possible.

I have won matches 6-0, 6-0. Unfortunately, I have also lost 0-6, 0-6, but not very often. Nevertheless, whenever you lose a match 0-6, 0-6, it is devastating. It is like no matter what you do or try, you cannot get out from under the power of your opponent. Life can sometimes seem like a never-ending losing match that there is no escape from. You must keep playing and trying like hell to win, but everything is conspiring against you to keep pushing you down, causing you to continue to feel like all is against you and there is no reprieve.

Constant defeat, continually coming at you, can cause you to feel like a failure, as though you have nothing left to offer and your life isn't worth a damn.

I can honestly say that I love tennis. I love playing, watching, practicing, and talking about it. There isn't much that I don't love about tennis. I find it interesting that losing in tennis (which is probably my least favorite aspect) is called love.

HEARTBREAK

When You Hear Hoofbeats, Don't Think Zebras

Everything seemed to combine into a breaking point in the fall of 2009. It had been nine years since I was diagnosed, and I thought I had made my peace with the diagnosis and come to a place where the disability was part of my life but didn't define or control me. I was working, had just gotten married, and felt things were going well and I had come to a calm place in my life.

However, on October 5, 2009, shortly before my 34th birthday, I was abruptly reminded that I did not control my body and it would and could at any moment wreak complete havoc. It started off simply enough.

After watching a just-released Michael Moore movie with my new husband, I felt my heart suddenly start to race as we walked to the car. In my daily life, an accelerated heartbeat happens frequently, at different times, and during all different activities. I usually don't notice it. Occasions like this, when I needed to sit down, were rare. Rob and I sat for a few moments on some nearby steps while I waited for my heart rate to decrease. After a few minutes, I no longer felt my heart racing, so we resumed our walk toward the car. I had only taken a few steps when I felt the racing heartbeat return. A nagging panic started to creep up, and my concern was quickly turning to fear.

I asked my husband to get the car, rather than trying to continue walking. We arrived home and I called my mom and told her what had happened, and she made the decision that we needed to contact the cardiologist on call.

I explained to him who I was, what had happened, and the fact that I had a pacemaker. When he responded with, "Why do you have a pacemaker?" I decided that I had no patience for this, especially since I hadn't wanted to call him in the first place, and handed the phone to my mother to explain.

Spitfire

My mother continued to give the doctor information about my diagnosis and why I had been given a pacemaker in 2004. I had been suffering from electrical issues in relation to my heart for several years and it was determined in 2004 that in order to be "protected," I needed to have one implanted. There hadn't been any issues for the last few years, but the feeling I had experienced that afternoon was more intense than anything I'd recently felt. Eventually, it was determined by the cardiologist that I needed to be seen and at the very least have an EKG done. As my mother was finishing her conversation with the cardiologist, it became clear that I would be spending the weekend in the hospital.

Although it had been a few years, this was not a new precedent since any time I had an "episode," I was placed in the hospital where I was "protected." My device was turned off; I was put on the telemetry floor and attached to a cordless monitor. It can be somewhat dramatic as I am usually one of the youngest and by far the healthiest people there. I have a lot of visitors and usually spend most of my time in the lounge or waiting room.

Unfortunately, I usually end up sharing a room with someone who seems either to be on the verge of death, or half dead already. All this has done for me is to convince me that not only do I not want to get old, but old and sick is a situation to be avoided at all costs. In these moments, my diagnosis weighs heavy on me.

A few weeks prior, at my cardiology appointment, I was told that the lead from my pacemaker to my ventricle had broken. Since most of my symptoms were atrial-related, this wasn't seen as a big problem. However, without this lead, they couldn't determine if my current symptoms were coming from my atrial chamber or my ventricle. (This is slightly important considering one kind is irritating, and the other, fatal).

When Monday finally rolled around and it was time to do something, I was told that either my lead would be replaced, or I would get an ICD implanted, a defibrillator and pacemaker combination. In basic terms, a device that would keep my heartbeat from going too slow and keep it from going too fast. If my heartbeat was too slow the pacemaker would pace it. If my heart went too fast the defibrillator would shock it back into a normal rhythm. I had numerous tests and discussions with a variety of doctors about options and procedures that could be performed.

This is a teaching hospital, which means that there are medical students and nurses that are doing their training and accompanying the cardiologist, or they may just come in on their own and want to "examine" me. This can happen over and over daily and get quite tiring.

I have some of my own rules that I adhere to. One is that I don't want to be examined more than twice a day. I understand this is the value of a teaching hospital and that I am a rare case which makes me more interesting, but having my heart listened to by anywhere from two to six people in a day and having them ask me the same questions over and over and over is not something that I feel I should have to be subjected to. Add that on to the fact that the nurses come every two hours to do vitals and all the other routines of the hospital, and it is easy to understand why this is so exhausting. My mother has, on occasion, barred people from my room and told them that I have been examined enough. I am more than happy to be a tool for learning and teaching but not to my own detriment.

On the morning of the procedure, four days after I was admitted, I was taken down to the OR at 6:50 AM. I woke up during the surgery, which was not expected, but due to not enough anesthesia. I was frightened, crying, and clinging to a nurse on my right side. There was such an enormous pressure on my left shoulder that felt like it would break off, although there was no pain. I believe the nurse on my right was there to keep me from moving or seeing what was happening on my left. I asked for Dr. Capeless (my cardiologist) and he waved at me to let me know where he was in a sea of masked doctors and nurses.

My mother had warned the anesthesiologist that I was only to be given the minimum amount of sedation possible. Due to having MD, I could easily die if given too much anesthesia since it suppresses breathing. To my way of thinking, being overdosed is seriously underrated, and I had no interest in being conscious during the upcoming procedure. I would take all the sedation I could get.

However, even more concerning to me, in response to my mother's warning, the anesthesiologist told us that this procedure would be quite unpleasant especially if I wasn't sedated enough. I still wasn't sure if I was only having my pacemaker lead replaced or getting an ICD. In hindsight, having been shocked by my defibrillator several times since when I was fully awake I think unpleasant is a huge understatement.

I've asked many cardiologists in electrophysiology if they have ever been shocked. None of them have. For police officers to carry tasers they must be tased first. This gives them an understanding of how it works, also what it feels like and how it affects someone. I believe doctors who oversee implanting these devices that may or may not cause unnecessary shocks to someone who is conscious should have to experience it as well.

My mother has always been very reticent in terms of using or doling out painkillers, anti-anxiety medication, or anti-depressants. She feels that pain is a good thing because it tells you something is wrong. In most cases, I already know what's wrong, and being in pain would make it harder for me to heal.

In my view, I am not at risk of becoming addicted or using drugs when I don't need them. There are times, especially when dealing with PTSD when anti-anxiety medication is necessary and helpful. I am not a huge fan of medication of any kind, especially anti-depressants but have realized that as a short-term form of relief, they work wonders. I tend to see this type of medication as a support to get "over the hump," and don't see it as something I will need long-term. My husband has been given the responsibility of making sure I get prescriptions for the needed medication when I am leaving the hospital, as my mom is not inclined to ask for anything. When all my friends received prescription painkillers for having their wisdom teeth out, I was given Tylenol.

On the day of my heart surgery, I had left my floor before 7 AM and didn't return until almost 11 PM. I spent many hours in the PACU (post-anesthesia care unit). I woke up shaking from head to toe and crying that I had to go to the bathroom and needed my catheter removed. I lay there trembling, whimpering, and calling out "please" to anyone who may be close enough to listen or care. Things were a bit hazy, which I am sure was a blessing.

My father came in with my husband to see me and say goodbye, as he needed to go home and rest. My husband sat with me for a few minutes until I asked him to leave. I felt so indescribably awful that I didn't want anyone to see me. So much of my time in the hospital is spent trying to reassure others that I am fine or feeling as though I have to entertain them that I exhaust myself.

This is a phenomenon felt by others during medical crises. In her book *"Brain on Fire,"* Cahalan describes: "I seemed to be able to somehow pull myself together when I had visitors, but it would often leave me depleted and as if I had devoted all my energy to acting normal" (Cahalan, 2012). After my surgery, I didn't feel the energy or strength to do anything except lie there in misery and I was uncomfortable subjecting my husband of just three months to this. I still felt that I had to reassure him, which I was unable to do in my current state.

After what seemed like hours, although time was a bit shifty, I asked the nurse to get my mother. She came in and requested warmed blankets (like they have in the ER) because I was obviously cold. I was shaking violently due to the anesthesia, the adrenalin I had been given during the procedure, and the residue of having the defibrillator tested after it was implanted.

My mother sat with me, holding onto my leg and her presence soothed me. I asked her if she thought my husband was hurt that I had asked for her and she assured me he wasn't. My mother washed my face and lips and made me as comfortable as possible.

One of my favorite and most comforting memories is of being at the Atlantic Ocean as a child. I would play in the water for hours and come out totally frozen with blue lips. My mother would wrap me in a big beach towel warm from the sun and hold me in her lap, which was warm as well. The feel of her warm body cradling mine is one of the most comforting feelings I ever remember having.

It is this comfort and soothing that can ease my fear. Whenever I would be scared as a child my mother would find a way to allay these fears. As I got older, I realized that many of the things she told me that made me less afraid or sounded perfectly reasonable didn't really make any sense, but they had worked at the time. My mother has been known to somewhat stretch or change the truth to keep me from being overly anxious about a situation.

Several hours later my husband rejoined me. I asked him to help me up to go to the bathroom. I objected when the nurse brought in a commode but soon realized that I couldn't even stand up, let alone walk. I continually overestimate what I (or my body) can do.

I returned to my room around 11 PM, and a nurse whom my mother had hired for the night showed up to be with me. Not a naturally verbose person, I couldn't stop talking.

I stayed up all night talking and trying to convince everyone that I would rather take the alternative to having an implant, even if that ended in death. They, of course, didn't believe me and tried to convince me otherwise, but I stand by my statement. Years later, when I told my friend Kelly that I wish I had never had my ICD implanted, even if it meant death, she cried.

I am always told that the decision to have or not have a medical procedure is my choice. To me, this seems ludicrous as I feel like I had no choice. Given that the alternative is death (which, in all honesty, seems the lesser of two evils sometimes) there is no way I can refuse a treatment that may save my life.

However, I am not making the choice for myself. I would rather live life on my terms and if that involves death, then that's the way it goes. The choice that I am making has to do with the wishes of my family, my husband, and all those who think the world is a better place with me around. Of course, they're right but that doesn't make all the pain, drama, and indignities any easier to swallow. It still feels like there is no choice involved. I was serious when I told the nurse that I would rather take my chances. This is not a new thought, but it has nothing to do with being suicidal. Even during my most "suicidal" times, during my deepest depression, it was not so much a desire to die, but more an intense desire for it all to STOP. I didn't want to die but I wanted to not have to live every day with the constant pain, the depression, the struggles, and finally, and most painful, the despair.

I was tired, so, so tired of having to be strong, of having to reassure everyone that I was fine, of trying to be upbeat and making others laugh, of spending all night in the hospital unable to sleep, and then feeling it wasn't fair to those who came to visit to sleep while they were visiting. One of the last times in the hospital, I asked my husband to get into bed and hold me, and finally, I was able to sleep.

The next morning, I met with a nurse practitioner and doctors to be discharged. The standard recovery for an implant surgery is two weeks, but it was decided that I would be out of work for six weeks. I couldn't believe it when my mother suggested it to the discharge nurse, considering that she is from the "walk it off" school of thought.

However, in the end, it wasn't even close to being enough. The ravages that had occurred in my life in the previous two years were so monumental and overwhelming that I ended up needing a three-month medical leave that summer.

Of course, this was only the beginning.

My Wish

I wish healthcare workers could understand the feeling of frustration, helplessness, and to some degree lack of self-importance when I am asked questions that could easily be ascertained by looking at my chart. I realize doctors are very busy and that they have a lot to do, but I don't have the patience or energy to explain it over and over every time I have a new doctor. It just simply makes me feel unimportant and as if I am a nuisance.

I experienced this again when I went into the hospital in the fall of 2011 due to complications from bronchitis. The doctor on call didn't even bother to read my chart before rounds and had no idea what medications I was on, why I was taking them, and what any pre-existing conditions were. I am not trained in medicine or healthcare, and I do not feel it is my job to educate healthcare workers every time I see them. My feeling is that medical professionals should have more information than I do.

When you have what is termed as a "rare" disease a shift occurs between the patient and the healthcare provider. In many cases, the patient is more knowledgeable and needs to be the educator. While the healthcare provider is the medical expert, the patient is the expert on themselves. Being ignored, dismissed, or being told the symptoms you are experiencing are basically in your head can be very frustrating and dismaying, especially when you aren't a hypochondriac and need answers.

"What used to be called a 'zebra' (in doctor parlance, a very rare disease) is now increasingly recognized..." (Cahalan, pg.251).

Whether a healthcare provider has any knowledge of your disease, or of you as a patient it is necessary for them to be willing to listen to you. Not reading the chart of a patient you are unfamiliar with is a similar issue. While they may lack the knowledge or understanding of what you are dealing with, it is exhausting to continually repeat yourself or deliver information that could easily be ascertained by a quick perusal of your already documented information.

Most often the case is that I know more about my situation than the healthcare provider does. Of course, it is a health situation that I am closely involved with and live with every day, but if I knew all the answers and was able to write prescriptions for myself, I wouldn't need a doctor in the first place. My primary care physician has suggested several times that I get a liver test done due to the enzymes that are being released. I have explained that this is unnecessary because in MD, the enzymes are from the muscles deteriorating. We always must be wary of tests and procedures because they can end up being detrimental or fatal when done for the wrong reasons.

HIGH HEELS
Age 36

I have a love affair with shoes. I must have 30 pairs of them, ranging from worn-out flip-flops to serious winter boots. There are dress shoes for summer, clogs, mud shoes, sandals, boots that reach almost to my knees, hiking boots, and athletic shoes. Shoes make the outfit is one of my guiding beliefs, and no shoes make an outfit like high heels. I love the way they look and the way they make me feel. Now, MMD has come between me and my high heels.

I've never been great at walking in heels, but now it is virtually impossible. Walking long distances is hard enough; strap a pair of heels on me and I can barely make it 10 feet. Over the past few years, I've accepted this, giving up any shoes that are too tall or too wobbly.

I've held onto a few pairs of my more "sensible" heels, but for the most part, they just gather dust in my closet, keepsakes to remind me of the fun times I had while wearing them. I will occasionally put on a pair to dress up an outfit for an outing. It takes the distance from my bedroom to the kitchen to remind me that I'm taking my life in my hands. Most likely, I won't even be able to make it to the car.

These days, if I wear platform shoes or wedges and don't completely focus, I will fall. Even crossing the room requires furniture surfing because I'm that unsteady. As for making it down the stairs, forget it. Wearing heels is a risky thing for me to do because if I fall and break a bone, I'm never getting those muscles back.

The last time I wore heels and had to walk any distance I had to lean most of my weight on my husband. He ended up practically having to carry me.

"Did you hurt your feet?" my mother asked when we returned.

"Only my toes," I responded.

"Well, your toes are a significant part of your feet," she helpfully pointed out.

I took the shoes off and rubbed my aching toes, longing for the days when I could manage to walk more than a few feet in my favorite sandals. But more than my feet hurt, strapping those shoes on changed my whole feeling about myself. I love opportunities to be dressed up. I want to show off my body and be seen as sexy, feminine, alluring, and womanly. For me, high heels represent so much more than just fashion or another pair of shoes. They were symbolic. Now my illness was forcing me to give up part of myself — my femininity - and that was a crushing blow.

As a little kid, my fondest wish was to be a boy. Being faster, stronger, and doing things even better than the boys became my goal and one that I usually attained. I was constantly active and never sat still for a minute. In second grade, my teacher would let me do cartwheels to the pencil sharpener, just to help me get the wiggles out.

Since I didn't end up becoming a boy, I decided that the next best thing was to beat the boys. When my male cousin and I would run around the block and I'd beat him by a long shot, I felt like I could conquer the world. I felt strong, in control, and just downright badass every time I won another tennis championship. This was Leslie, the extraordinary athlete: extremely competitive, active, lively, determined, and in control — and I loved this me. When my self-regard wavered during my teenage years, this was the self-image I would draw upon and it would lift me back up.

When I was six or seven years old, my three cousins from Long Island came to visit for a week. My mother, never one to have kids sitting around all day, signed all of us up for a sports camp from eight to noon every day. She would drop us off in the morning at the high school with a bag lunch and our bathing suits. After the camp, we would have our lunch and then walk to the town pool and swim until the pool closed at 5 PM. When my mom returned to pick us up, we would all be sitting on the curb exhausted.

The activities picked up right where they'd left off when it was our turn to go to Long Island. My mother took my brother, me, and the three cousins on a canoe trip. We spent the entire day canoeing around a reservoir, exploring, racing back and forth, and having a wonderful time.

There was always an activity, a game, or adventure, and all of it involved being physically active. I ran, jumped, hiked, and swam. I rode horseback, did gymnastics, played Little League, and wrestled. Most of my summers were spent at the beach. I'd stay all day, every day, coming home only to have lunch and change my bathing suit. I spent hours in the water, and when I was back on dry land, I was playing soccer, wiffle ball, paddle tennis, tag, or some game we just made up.

As I got a little older, I turned to more serious sports. There was tennis, of course, but also sailing, field hockey, ice skating, and ski racing. I loved them all and went to every camp I could. In high school, I played three varsity sports a year, and in the winter, I would figure skate before and have ski practice after school. When I wanted to work out with the guys on the ski team on Sundays, my mother, a coach with a very strong attitude about the value of exercise, put her fist down.

"You can't exercise more than six days a week."

I never thought about calories, gaining weight, or dieting. I had very little body fat and didn't have enough to start my period or completely go through puberty until I was 16. Even when I did gain a few pounds in high school after I quit field hockey, I lost it all in a matter of days, as soon as I started exercising again. During high school, my friend and I would go out to dinner once a week.

Since I love potatoes of any kind, I would always order a baked potato and French fries. It never occurred to me that this was a lot of calories. Through my senior year of high school, I used a rice cooker in my room for most of my meals. If I knew what carbohydrates were, I never gave them a thought. It wasn't until several years after college that I started to put on weight.

I've been trying to lose weight ever since, with little or no success. Of all the things my disability has taken from me, my inability to get back the body I had before has been among the most demoralizing. My cravings for carbohydrates are as intense as when I was a teen, but now I can't burn those calories through exercise, or even exercise much at all.

To have lost the body I once loved and was proud of was hard. Losing abilities that I had never given much thought to, such as standing on my toes, was like a slap in the face.

"What's wrong?" my friend asked, when she found me in the kitchen, crying to my mother.

"I can't stand on my toes anymore," I said through my tears.

She looked at me in confusion. "Why do you need to stand on your toes?"

I tried to explain that it wasn't that I needed to stand on my toes; it was the fact that I couldn't do it anymore. I'd walked and even run on my toes for most of my life and now I couldn't. It was another sign that the muscles that held me up — in this case, my feet and ankle muscles - were weakening. It was another thing that MMD had taken from me.

Today, I can stand on my toes only if I hold onto something. This skill, which seems so silly, is one that I wanted to keep. Being unable to shift my weight onto my toes means no more jumping. I can't do jumping jacks or jump rope. Even walking in a normal manner, which requires shifting your weight from heel to toe, is affected. The summer when I was 35, I noticed I now make a lot of noise when I walk, especially when I come down the stairs. It means I now walk on my heels and was an ominous sign of what was to come. When my brother and my father began to fall, they would fall backward. Neither had been up on their toes in years.

PLEIOTROPY
Colin - Present

At this point my brother Colin's symptoms are physically more severe than mine. While we both experience limitations, his affect his life to a greater extent than mine do. To some extent, I can live my life the way I want. While we have many of the same symptoms, we also have different ones. I manifest the cardiac symptoms of MMD most severely, while his primary manifestation is the muscle features. This is a case of pleiotropy, a feature of MMD.

In addition, we have different personalities and attitudes and approach most things from different perspectives. To this day, my brother will stay up until he literally falls asleep. He won't and basically can't get up at a reasonable hour, and the theory is that he lacks the motivational factor that causes most people to get up and be productive. Why get up if there isn't anything you want to do?

My brother is unable to live independently. Even though I depend on my husband and my mother to help support me, I can do many more activities, both of daily living and exercise, than my brother can. If I want to get a coffee, go for a walk, do sea glass collecting, or indulge my significant shopping habit, I can do so without any trouble. While I must plan out my day in a way that works, for the most part, I can do what I want. I can accomplish what I want to get done which gives me more flexibility than my brother has. Granted, I also have a lot more things I want to do. Usually, I do more by the time my brother gets up in the morning than he does all day.

Colin experiences much more lower body issues, he must lock his knees with every step he takes and if he loses his balance or trips, he falls. He has no quad muscles, so getting him up when he falls is challenging, as he must get his legs under him before he can stand. When he falls, he goes down like a ton of bricks and has broken many small pieces of furniture, several toes, and both his patellas. He is tall and overweight which makes him quite heavy, so my mother and I are unable to get him up by ourselves. If he falls during the night, he must crawl to the couch and stay there until my mother gets up and can assist him.

One of the arguments I have had with both my mother and brother is that when he falls, he needs to call rescue for a lift assist rather than relying on my mom. My mother, while being strong, is in her late seventies and quite tiny. If he falls on her he could kill her. My mother relies on various neighbors and an occasional stranger off the street to assist her in getting him up. I know my mother, under pain of death, will not call rescue for any reason. I have told Colin it is his responsibility to call, but as with most things, he defers to my mother.

Colin struggles going up or down stairs to the point where it is close to impossible. He can only do it if there are two very strong railings that extend past the start of the stairs. The same is true of ramps, or curbs, which means he must find a cut curb to cross the street and is often unable to use ramps to enter stores or other places that claim to be "handicapped accessible."

Colin shared with me, "I'm concerned that I'll eventually get to the point where I am unable to take care of myself. More worried that I am going to get to the point where I am not going to be able to live on my own and take care of myself."

In my case, my lower body is much less affected, although this could change at any moment. There are things we might have done differently had we known this disease was coming down the line. One of the best things we could have done was to be extremely active as children and build up a large muscle mass. Coincidently we both did this, without knowing that it would be to our great benefit.

Seeing how we both have very different symptoms that manifested in different ways there is no way to say one has it "worse" than the other. For us both, the struggle is trying to get through the activities of daily living to the best of our abilities.

My disease is slowly causing my muscles to deteriorate. Because of the extreme athleticism of my youth, the strong muscles I developed then are helping to protect me now. It is the muscles I formed as a child, chasing a field hockey ball, or lunging for a volley on the tennis court that allows me to walk today and to get where I need to go and carry out the activities of day-to-day living that I would otherwise be unable to do. Without that muscle base, I would most likely be far less mobile today. The conundrum I face is that keeping that muscle requires exercise, but if I exercise too much, I'll damage the muscles I have left. Don't exercise too much, sounds like advice that shouldn't be too hard to follow, but being competitive and determined is part of my very nature. I often end up over-exercising for someone in my condition. Then I am done in for the rest of the day and for days afterward.

My husband and I have a code phrase for those days when it's impossible for me to even get out of bed. I'm simply too tired to go on. The kind of fatigue that you feel at the end of a long day? That's typically how I feel when I get up in the morning. Think about how you feel when you've only gotten a few hours of sleep. Now imagine trying to go two full days in a row without any rest, or only sleeping every other night. For most people, one good night's sleep is enough to counteract a bad one. I'm not so lucky. I pay the price for a sleepless night for about a week.

WHAT YOU CAN EXPECT

Every year since 2001, my family goes to Baltimore to have our annual checkup with our team of doctors. These include a neurologist, cardiologist, and pulmonologist. In addition to seeing these three doctors, each specialty comes with its own battery of tests. Since this is usually accomplished in one marathon day, it is beyond exhausting. It's about an 8–10-hour drive and in the last few years we have either split the drive up by spending Saturday night in New York with my extended family or driving down the whole way on Saturday in order to have a day to recover. I hate everything about these trips. Every year I vow that I'm not going, but in the end, I don't really have a choice.

I can't help but to look at these yearly visits with anxiety. It is a pretty "in your face" view of reality, and not an entirely welcome focus on something that I do my best not to dwell on and wallow in. Often the visits go without a hitch, but it is the unexpected results that make me, (and all of us), apprehensive. The fact that in years past I have gone there thinking everything is fine and ended up with a pacemaker certainly weighs on my mind. Or a few years ago when I was placed on a medication that caused me to have ventricular tachycardia and experience the extreme nightmare sensation of my defibrillator going off, followed by the traumatic event of having it happen again a few hours later, where the result was an ambulance ride to the hospital.

Whenever I have gained a significant amount of weight in the year leading up to the appointment, I am sure to get read the riot act. I know that those of us with MMD are not only susceptible to metabolic syndrome, which I clearly have as my weight is centered on and around my middle but also, as a bonus, diabetes. Clearly not something I am interested in tacking on to my already somewhat lengthy laundry list of problems, ailments, and medical issues.

I don't like talking about what may be wrong with me and what parts of my body may be deteriorating or not working, as they should be. When someone makes even an innocuous comment about my condition or symptoms it can easily make me angry. I do my best to not exactly face all that is wrong with me and avoid doing things that bring it into sharp relief. This is not to say that I take the ostrich approach to my condition. I try to fight the good fight and focus on what I can do daily to make myself healthy and strong. I am fighting a losing battle, but I believe it is much better to at least attempt to fight rather than stick my head in the sand and completely give up.

My family is on the positive end of the MMD spectrum. Since none of us has congenital MMD we are pretty much able to function to a certain extent. Since my father had adult-onset MMD and my brother and I both had adolescent onset, for many years of our lives none of us experienced anything but the mildest symptoms. We all have different symptoms that we struggle with to a various degree but do not have the difficulties and tragedies of a child born with congenital MMD, resulting in extreme disability.

In some ways, we are seen as not having much of a disability compared to the population that is usually being seen. However, this is not as positive of a situation as it might seem. We are still stuck in a hospital for at least eight hours, shuttling between various doctors in a variety of specialties, all to see what ground we have lost in the last year. We are subjected to numerous tests and procedures, some more painful or challenging than others. We see doctors, fellows, technicians, and medical students.

The first year my brother and I met with genetic counselors whose main job was to share the staggering and depressing statistical facts about our condition with us. Basically, what I took away from this was that our life expectancy was mid-fifties; cataracts were coming soon, and a whole host of other unpleasantness. As with most devastating events the details fade but the overall impressions stay remarkably clear. Over the years I have mostly forgotten what they said but am still stuck with an impression that they seemed so cavalier in delivering this life-altering and dreadful news. Obviously, this left a bad taste in my mouth.

My wish is that the news would have been delivered like this:

"The information that we have to share with you is based on statistics of the previous generation. There have been many improvements in the understanding of this disease and patient care. These are also symptoms that may or may not affect you. What we have seen in the past in patients with adolescent-onset can be somewhat attributed to lack of knowledge and misdiagnoses. There are some symptoms that we commonly see, such as cataracts, cardiac issues, and facial features. The risk of developing secondary complications are higher than in the general populations, such as a high risk of developing diabetes."

Giving us information in a positive and respectful manner would have been much preferable.

Being female, I got to have more interaction with genetic counselors on the topic of having children. While my brother carries the gene he is as likely to pass it on as I am, but due to the many complications, pregnancy can cause in "normal" people the risks would be much higher for me. Seeing a genetic counselor that was closer to my age and was also colleagues with my good friend Kelly, made it easier to discuss the options and challenges of trying to have children.

A few years later, as a bonus, I got to see a social worker. As a social worker myself I was excited at this prospect, and I enjoy meeting other professionals in my field. However, this turned out to be a vast disappointment.

The social worker started the conversation by asking me if I had ever met a social worker. As I've mentioned, being condescended to is the quickest way to get me extremely irritated, lose any interest in being polite, and resort to heavy sarcasm. Did she really think I had reached my mid-thirties and never met a social worker? In addition, this woman had full access to my chart and could have looked up ahead of time to see what my profession was. However, I decided to give this woman the benefit of the doubt.

"I have met several social workers, and I'm actually a social worker myself."

"What kind of social work do you do?"

"Currently, I work with Developmentally Disabled adults, but I am interested in hospital social work. I'm hoping to get my license soon."

She then, quite rudely responded, "In Baltimore, if you don't have your license, you can't call yourself a social worker."

She really was going a little too far, telling me what I could and couldn't call myself.

To this, I replied, "In Vermont, you can call yourself anything you want. In order to test you need to be on the unlicensed registry for two years. Also, since I'm not doing clinical work, I'm unable to get the supervision I need."

"Well, if you are not doing clinical work and you don't have your license, you're not really a social worker."

This was way too much, and I figured the only course of action I had was to continue to let her spout complete nonsense and get out of there as quickly as possible. Was meeting with this woman supposed to be a benefit to me?

We didn't get off on the right foot and the meeting didn't get any better as it continued. She pointed out to me that my claim that even making dinner was a serious challenge was certainly exaggerated since you could buy precut vegetables and cooking some protein took very little effort. This woman was intolerable! She was acting as though now that I knew I could buy precut vegetables all my problems were solved. I was happy to get some help with suggestions to make my life easier, but I had an overwhelming sense of frustration, irritation, and helplessness at the lack of acknowledgment of my struggles. It is hard enough to experience life struggles, but to then feel like no one believes you is infuriating. This was where the meeting went from bad to worse. When I received my follow-up visit notes, I learned she had the case notes and diagnosis of someone else, who suffered from a completely different disease and had no relationship to my situation or me at all. This really was the very last straw.

Moving on from telling me that my life wasn't too bad she totally shifted gears and started talking to me about how hard my life was. As I have said before, compassion does a lot for me, but all sympathy does is make me feel sorry for myself, which is the last thing I need help with.

What You Can Expect

  Later, when talking to my doctor I asked her who had hired this social worker. She said she had and after I gave her my reaction to the social worker's complete incompetence and lack of professionalism, she asked me if I thought she should fire her. Her behavior and inability to relate to this population was inexcusable, and it didn't seem like a good fit to say the least.

TILT

When the onset of my major MMD symptoms occurred sometime during my late adolescence I mainly felt confusion. I couldn't understand the changes in my body and why I was losing abilities that were second nature. I did not know where these troubling and challenging issues were coming from. There was no way for me to determine not only how to deal with the early symptoms but to identify what was causing them. I constantly, and sometimes daily, go through the stages of grief.

Depression had been part of my life for many years and was to come back again and again with great force. Leaving home and the public school system to attend a private boarding school in Connecticut seemed to coincide with the onset of my early MMD symptoms. Adolescence on its own is challenging in the best of circumstances, which this definitely wasn't. Adding a new environment, challenging academics, extremely competitive sports, and a whole new social situation to the fatigue that was emerging were beyond my capabilities.

MMD contributed to my struggles, and I felt completely betrayed by my body. At that point, I still had my abilities, but my recovery time was much longer. I could no longer run long distances but for the most part, things were relatively unchanged. I could play field hockey for hours and I loved sprints, but the distance runs at the beginning of practice were hell and almost impossible. At the beginning of the field hockey season, the running requirement was just one lap around the three practice fields, but any sustained running was no longer something I could do with any regularity.

Later in the season, the requirement became two laps. Any activity that stopped and started or required short bursts of speed was my forte. Anything that required sustained movement such as running for a long distance was something I could no longer do easily. This was the first time I couldn't just power through some activity that was challenging. I quit field hockey partway through my senior year because I couldn't complete the warm-up run and I was always exhausted.

Three-hour tennis matches or eight hours of skiing were no problem—until the next day. These two sports were different from running because they don't require constant or consistent or repetitious movement. In tennis, there is some sprinting, and you are constantly moving, but you stop and start. Skiing is also a physical sport but there is the chairlift ride up and gravity and the slope pulling you forward. For this same reason, I loved Indian sprints, which everyone else felt was a punishment. Changing speeds was something I could do and do well.

I couldn't run long distances to save my life. I could force myself through it to a point and then I was unable to keep going. And there was no explanation for this. I don't think I have ever been angrier—and depression is anger turned inward.

I never moved through the stages of grief in a linear way, and I still go through them constantly. Every time a new symptom appears or I have a new pain or struggle, I start with denial and anger, skip over bargaining, and head right for depression. Even thinking too much about the struggles, hurdles, and detriments of my disability can lead me into a downward spiral.

Acceptance is hard-won and can fade almost as soon as it is achieved. Although I had experienced them previously my real intimacy with the stages of grief occurred at the age of 25 when I received my diagnosis. This would be my first stage, the stage of denial. I felt fine (even though I had been searching for a diagnosis for the struggles I was experiencing) and since the only symptom I really had been dealing with was fatigue, then nothing serious was wrong.

I was quickly disabused of this notion when I ended up in the hospital a few months later, shortly before Christmas of 2000, a month after diagnosis. I had a few episodes of passing out or feeling like I was going to faint at work. The first time this happened, I had gone by ambulance to the hospital, where my parents met me a few hours later. After several tests the doctor informed my parents that I had heart block. This greatly upset my mother, who told the doctor he was wrong, and we left shortly after. Due to this incident, I had to have a stress test.

My father brought me to the hospital for this test and, having had a few stress tests himself, gave me an overview of what I could expect. My blood pressure would be taken, lying down, sitting, and then standing to see how it changed. Then I would walk or run on a treadmill to see if my heart replicated the symptoms that had been causing me to faint. It seemed easy and straightforward. A minute into the test the cardiologist pulled me off the treadmill and sat me down on the bed. He told me to lie down and had the nurse take my blood pressure. He said my heart rate had shot up to over 300 beats a minute. I hadn't felt a thing. This didn't seem to be too alarming to me, especially since I hadn't felt anything.

Later, telling my mother on the phone, she freaked out. She couldn't believe that I hadn't felt the racing heartbeat and was very concerned about this information. I was happy, my dad was in Burlington with me, and we were eating Japanese food. After the stress test, he had taken me to my favorite restaurant, and I was enjoying being with him. All was good in my world, and since I hadn't felt the racing heartbeat I figured how bad could it be? If it wasn't causing me pain, then it obviously wasn't something to worry about.

A few days later, my boyfriend picked me up at work in the middle of the day after my boss had called him and told him I had just experienced extreme dizziness. He dropped me off at home and went back to work. My mother called later in the afternoon. When I answered the phone, she asked me why I wasn't at work. I told her what had happened and that I decided to come home. She called back a few minutes later to tell me that she had called my boyfriend to come pick me up and take me to the hospital, where we would meet with my cardiologist.

I had been seeing a cardiologist for the last seven years since at age 18, I had been diagnosed with a heart murmur. It was no big deal, and all that was required was occasional EKGs and echocardiograms. Obviously, something else was going on.

I don't remember the exact sequence of events, but to my dismay, shortly after I arrived, I was informed that I would be spending the night in the hospital. I couldn't really figure out what everyone was so worried about because as usual, I felt fine. My roommate Jen had come to the hospital with me, and she went back to our apartment with my mother to pick up a few things for me while my dad and I stayed at the emergency room.

I then had the pleasure of getting an IV inserted which was done so poorly that I was screaming in pain and begging the technician to remove it. He very nonchalantly said it was already in and if he removed it, he would have to do it again. I told him he was lucky my mother wasn't there. She can be quite fierce. During the time I was in the hospital, my mother had grabbed my cardiologist by the lapels of his lab coat and made it clear that he was to do whatever he needed to keep me safe.

I was very upset that I had to stay at the hospital, and after the disastrous IV, I was even less enthusiastic. I was still in a lot of pain from the IV, and I was soaked with sweat due to my pain and anxiety about what was actually going on. However, I eventually was put into a room on the telemetry floor, started watching TV and settled in for the evening.

The next morning my mother was there when I woke up. I was happy to see her as I had a very hard time sleeping and was a little worried because no one had really told me what, exactly, was wrong.

My dad showed up a little later in the morning. He sat down next to me, took my hand, and told me that he loved me very much. Then he started crying. He got up and walked out of the room to compose himself. This really scared me. I had seen both my parents cry before, but it was a very rare occurrence, and the situation didn't seem serious enough to warrant it.

I found out much later that my father felt like all that was happening to me was his fault since my problems were like his and had passed to me genetically through him. I asked my mother what was going on and she just said very calmly that he was worried about me. She has always been good about remaining calm in front of me, no matter what is going on.

If my mother can slightly alter the truth to make it more palatable, she will. A few days before my wedding my dad was in the hospital due to neck pain and trouble walking.

When I found out he was in the hospital I called my mother in a panic. She told me he just had a slight cold.

When I was 16, I had bronchial pneumonia and I was quite ill. My mother took my temperature and when I asked what it was, she said it was 103 degrees. I knew this wasn't good, but I felt too sick to care. She gave me some Advil and an hour later my dad took my temperature. He said, thankfully, that it had gone down. I asked him what it was, and he said 104. This was yet another example of my mother downplaying a negative situation and my father being truthful.

Eventually, I learned that the doctor had admitted me to the hospital because he was concerned that I wouldn't live through the weekend, and if I were in the hospital I would be protected. Later that day some of my mother's brothers and sisters came up from New York as well as my cousin who is a doctor. Another thing my mother is very good at is rallying the troops when there is a crisis. My friends came to visit me, and my mom gave my friend Jen her credit card to get me pajamas and underwear at Victoria's Secret. This was my first experience of exhausting myself by spending all my time assuring everyone else that I was okay.

On Monday morning after a long wait I was taken to a room to do another stress test to see if they could replicate the rapid heart rate. I was tired and not that interested in running on the treadmill. The doctor threatened that if I didn't keep running, he would get my mother, who had earlier offered to pick up my running sneakers. Eventually, he let me stop and scheduled a procedure for the next morning.

Since my heart hadn't replicated the rapid heartbeat, they decided to do an electrophysiology procedure to try again. I was scheduled for an electrophysiology (EP) study. The electrical current that controlled my heartbeat was what was being examined.

My aunt, who was visiting, was giving me information about the study as she herself had had the procedure before. When she got to the part about how they were going to shave my bikini line, my mother stopped her and told her I didn't need to know everything, another case of her trying to protect me. I was happy to get the information. In a hospital, I feel it's always better to have more information rather than less. Again, my mother feels like if I don't know how much something is going to suck, I won't worry about it as much.

Basically, I was told that a wire would be inserted into my femoral artery in my groin and fed into my heart. Then, an electrical current would be sent to see if my heart would go into a fast rhythm.

It's a bit surreal to be walking, talking, and wearing anything other than a hospital gown while being taken to surgery to have your heart shocked by a wire.

After the procedure was done and I was being wheeled back to my room, my mother came and told me it had gone well.

Apparently, despite being given adrenalin and having electrical currents shock my heart, it hadn't done anything worrisome, and the following day I was released from the hospital. I went back a few days later to do a tilt table test to see if that affected me in an informative way. Basically, you lie down on your back on a gurney and they strap a blood pressure cuff to your arm that automatically takes your blood pressure every minute or so. They also monitor your heart rate. Then they raise the table almost completely vertically. The clock was right in front of me, and I knew watching the minutes slowly go by was going to make everything feel that much longer.

I asked the nurse how long this would take, and she said about 40 minutes. This seriously sucked as I had long since noticed that it was uncomfortable for me to stand still in one place for very long. It made me feel nauseous. I remember always thinking that I wouldn't do well as a checkout girl having to stand all day in front of the register. I also had the same feeling when I kneeled in church. I had told my mother that, but she just thought I was trying to get out of going to mass. Usually, if I felt this way, I sat down and felt better. I didn't feel lightheaded or get head rushes from standing up too fast. However, drinking or smoking while standing up often made me feel sick. I didn't know this was a problem; I just figured it was another weird symptom of being me.

After about two minutes into the test, the nurse suddenly dropped the table backward and rushed up to me, asking if I was okay. I told her I didn't feel so well, which was a common occurrence of mine while standing still. She said she wasn't surprised I didn't feel well, as my blood pressure had dropped through the floor. The doctor had gone out to tell my mom that the test had been positive. When he saw the look on her face he assured her that this was a good thing because they now knew what was wrong with me and why I kept feeling dizzy and fainting. This was one of the few cases when getting a positive result was better than getting a negative result. A new symptom of my diagnosis was vasovagal syncope.

Since denial that anything was wrong with me was clearly no longer an option I swiftly moved into anger and decided that if my life was not going to go as planned and my choices had been taken away from me then I wouldn't miss any experiences. I felt that since there were many things that are certainties in people's lives that were no longer part of mine, I was going to live to the fullest. However, as with most decisions made in anger this was not the best plan. Looking back there were many experiences that I would have loved to miss, and several that I should have missed, but at this point in time shortly after my diagnosis, I was driven by anger and determined to make the most of whatever time I had left. I commenced to all sorts of destructive behavior that I didn't completely grow out of until my early 30s.

Things began to look up when I was 26 and accepted to graduate school in social work. I managed to graduate with a 3.8, but I continued my reckless behavior. It seemed I was trying to outrun my diagnosis and possibly myself as well. It was a classic case of denial. And boy, was I angry!

No matter what I did, where I went, or how far I tried to run, my diagnosis still crept up on me. My classrooms in graduate school were all on the 4th floor. Every day of class, I would walk up these four sets of stairs, arriving at the top breathless, sheet white, and looking as though I might expire on the spot. I was trying so hard to prove that I could do anything anyone else could. Some of it was pride, and some of it was me fighting against my diagnosis. I didn't want to stand out or have anyone wonder what was wrong with me or, even worse, pity me.

Graduate school helped me to be more willing to accept myself as I was and not to spend so much time and energy trying to fight against myself. A few of my classmates pointed out to me that I should take the elevator, which from them on I did. Slowly, I began to let my disability dictate more of my decisions in a positive rather than negative way. It became less important to do something just to prove that I could, such as taking the stairs. The elevator was symbolic for me. The longer I could take the stairs the longer I could delude myself into thinking that I was the same as everyone else and "normal." Finally, I was able to realize that I was hurting rather than helping myself and that anyone who saw me when I reached the top of the stairs would easily be able to see that the stairs weren't an easy challenge for me.

I went skiing one day with my mother during my first year of graduate school. The next day I was horrified to discover I couldn't walk up the stairs. It was not that I struggled with the stairs; I literally could not walk up them. This traumatized me, as it was one of those cases that you can't possibly ignore as anything other than a full-blown symptom. Being tired and feeling fatigued walking after strenuous exercise was a situation I could attribute to something else or just figure I had overdone it. I was still able, for the most part, to make my body do what I asked. This was something new, something I couldn't power through even though I tried my hardest. It terrified me.

Different activities that I had never thought about became harder and harder for me, and I struggled to pretend that I could still do them, although the effort was enormous. One of the things my friends and I did a lot during this time was dancing at the bars after class and on the weekends.

Previously, I could dance the whole night without a problem, and now, after dancing for at most one song I would need to sit down and rest. I would be utterly exhausted before the end of the evening; I couldn't stay out with everyone until the bars closed, and couldn't walk back to campus where I had left my car. Often, I would dispatch my boyfriend to get my car and walk home with a girlfriend who lived much closer to where we were. However, this walk required me to stop and rest at least once, and often her boyfriend would come to pick us up.

It was the loss of these abilities and ease and the experience that everyone goes through as they age. However, I wasn't very aged, and I had to deal with these struggles at a time way before everyone else.

Although my anger would fade for a time, it would always come back with a vengeance, and I would hear the voice in my head telling me again I was worthless, no good, and that nobody would ever want me. The war between anger and depression was waged daily, each one determined to get the best of me.

They say that one hundred compliments and achievements can be washed away in an instant by one negative or derogatory comment. With the way I was feeling about myself, I instinctively searched out those who would treat me the way I felt I deserved. I would settle for any kind of company to avoid being alone and could only spend very little time by myself before I had an overwhelming need to go somewhere or find someone so I wouldn't have to be alone with myself, my feelings, my doubts, fears, and insecurities. I loved graduate school, but this was a very tumultuous period and not a bright time in my life.

However, it did give me the forum to begin to examine what I was facing and have a way to gain an understanding. My final project for graduate school was on the psychosocial implications of adolescent-onset disability. I interviewed others with what I termed an "invisible disability," a disability that dictated a lot of your own life but was invisible to others and had started in adolescence. I interviewed one individual who had struggled with epilepsy, a girl recently diagnosed with Lupus, and another girl who had struggled with severe depression for many years. I could relate to them all and felt such validation and a very strong connection.

Through personal interviews and reading first-person accounts, I found the ability and words to tell my own story, from the first symptom to diagnosis and beyond. It was an amazing process. The interviewee and I would feel a mutual sense of relief in finding another who understood, on a basic level, what we were going through. Being able to explore several accounts through interviews, books, and research gave me the comforting sense that I was not alone and others had gone through struggles that resonated with mine. It wasn't even about acceptance. It was about finding a way to make my life work in this world and locate a pinprick of light in the darkness. Journaling and writing have always been a way for me to sort out, examine, and gain an understanding of my feelings. This was one of the biggest blessings I could have found.

    I was always searching for acceptance in any form I could. Acceptance of me, acceptance from others, and most of all the grace to stop my reckless angry behavior, escape my smothering depression, and accept my life in a new, redefined way. It is interesting to me that I am extremely accepting of others and so much less accepting of myself. My friend Kelly often tells me that my best attribute is being the most non-judgmental person she knows who sees the best in people and accepts them no matter their flaws. I feel that others have a more valid reason for their struggles than I do and can easily accept them but have trouble finding acceptance for myself. As if I am better or stronger or should just get over it. I know acceptance but have to find it several times a day.

    Without a doubt, acceptance is the hardest stage for me. The realization that I can be as accepting as possible and still be overwhelmed by grief is a tough one. Realizing that I am going to deal with loss and work towards acceptance every day of my life makes me feel so tired at times that I could cry. Waking up every day in pain and with crushing fatigue is acceptance in itself. Does this familiarity with grief make it any easier to reach acceptance? No way, no how.

PART FOUR

SERVING AND RECEIVING SERVE

SERVING AND RECEIVING SERVE

Often when I am playing tennis with my mom, she'll have me work on returning her serve. As she takes her backswing, I get my chair moving and try to read the direction in which the serve will be coming. While I move towards the ball, it rockets past me. "Good serve," I called out. I spent most of the time watching the ball go right past me, occasionally connecting but mostly missing or hitting a very weak return. Her serve is hard, fast, and able-bodied, but I tried to adjust to the challenge. For many years I tried to be an equal player to my mother. I finally got there and was able to match her power for power. Now that's all been stripped away, but as I sit in my wheelchair running down her serves and shots, I can feel that old power and force. Even if I can no longer generate it and even if I can't return it I can face any serve she sends my way.

During alternating games in tennis, one player is serving, and the other is receiving. Each player serves every other game. In able-bodied tennis, the server has the advantage and is expected to win their service games. In wheelchair tennis, it is the opposite because it is difficult to have as much strength in a serve while sitting. This highlights a major difference in the two forms of tennis.

The receiver must determine how to deal with the serve. The better the return of serve, the more likely to win the point, or at least to get your opponent off balance. Since the server starts the point, they are in somewhat of a stationary position while the receiver is moving. Getting a chair moving from a dead or near stop is much more difficult than continuing to move.

There are many parallels between the game of tennis and the game of life. Receiving service can be equated to rolling with, accepting, and preparing for life's punches. It is about taking what's coming, facing it, and finding a way to handle it, work with it, and shift it to your advantage.

Winning your service games or holding serve can be paralleled with holding your own in life. Balance in all areas of life is important. The more off-balance you are, the more difficult it becomes to regain it. Finding ways to make my life work and have balance is a daily struggle. To be able to do the things that are important to me and achieve the goals I've set for myself can be extremely challenging and is a constant work in progress.

A quote that resonates with me is "we can strive to be the best version of ourselves" (the champion's mind pg.7). I strive to be the best version of myself and to make my life the best version of the life that I have imagined. This isn't easy, and it all becomes much more difficult when I'm exhausted beyond all reason.

FAMILY RELATIONSHIPS

Family relationships are complicated and complex, mainly because you can't choose the members of the family you are born into. Whether you have a wonderful and supportive family, as is the case for me, or you have no family to speak of or you have no family you speak to, these are important and formative relationships.

I have had a loving, close, and special relationship with both of my parents. With my brother, it's not so simple. There are times when we join forces to achieve a common goal, support each other, and bond. One such example is on our annual family trip to Johns Hopkins. This is not a fun experience for any of us and not something we look forward to, except with trepidation. It starts out with an eight-hour drive to Baltimore, starting very early in the morning with an extremely tense mother. We have learned through the years that the most successful family trips tend to involve one or both of us using headphones. Being part of a conversation can often lead to the drive being even more stressful. Offering an opinion or advice when we get lost or miss an exit never leads anywhere positive, so we (especially me) usually try to tune out and not get involved.

A few years ago, as we got ready to leave, my brother tripped and hurt his ankle. He sat in the backseat so he was able to elevate his leg. I had planned to sit in the back and watch movies on my computer, but now I was in the front seat, meaning I was supposed to help navigate. One of the main drawbacks of not being able to tune out is my mother and brother's incessant arguing. This seems to be their favorite way of communicating with each other.

"Did you get the sailing schedule for the Burlington waterfront?"

"I called, but they didn't have the schedule done yet."

"Did you ask when they might have it or ask them to call you back when it's ready?"

"No."

"Why not?"

It's at this point that I usually interrupt and tell my mother to stop beating a dead horse.

"He did or didn't do whatever he did or didn't do, so can you please move on!" Being in the front means I get a front-row seat to these kinds of conversations.

They will go around and around, never agreeing and each trying to get the last word. My mother asks continuous leading questions, and my brother is constantly trying to defend himself or his course of action. Being a captive audience in these situations is beyond annoying.

My mother is very distrustful of her car's navigation system, Google maps, or Siri. During a previous trip, we were using the navigation system, both my and her iPhones, and were somewhere in New Jersey when she freaked out. She started yelling at my brother to find a map on his android phone, to which he protested that he didn't have the app because she didn't want to pay for it. Since she pays for their shared phone plan, she hadn't let him get it.

We pulled into a rest area as my mother continued to insist she was being led astray. Since the navigation system and both iPhones were all saying the same thing, I figured they were giving us the correct information, but in these situations, it tends to be better to keep your thoughts to yourself. When she finally calmed down enough to be coherent, I asked her why she thought that all the systems we had were against her.

"Mom, all the navigation systems are all saying the same thing. I don't understand why you think they are giving you misinformation."

She replied, "we just weren't going the way I know or the way we usually go." Incredulously I asked her, "If you know how to get there, why aren't we just going that way?"

Often when my mother acts this way, my brother and I find it quite amusing, and it usually makes us laugh. The more hyper she gets, the more we laugh and joke between ourselves.

When my father was alive, the drive was broken up into two days, with a stopover in New York on the way down to make the drive less exhausting. I always wanted to make the trip as short as possible but was overruled. However, this worked well because my parents could chat while my brother and I entertained ourselves. Now my brother usually sits in the front, so I can tune out in the back.

In January of 2016, I lost my father. This was a crushing blow, although I, unlike my other family members, had been urging my father to "let go." His quality of life was greatly diminished, and even though most of his organs were functioning, his lungs had been damaged to the point where he was no longer able to breathe on his own and in order to survive, he would have needed to be intubated which would have been devastating for him as well as for my mother. The last two days of his life, he struggled to hang on while we gathered around him and prepared for our final goodbyes. My mother stayed with him at night, and during the day, my brother, my husband, and I kept vigil.
I would sit next to him on the bed and hold his hand.
"Daddy, do you know how much I love you?"
My father could no longer talk, but he made eye contact, and I knew he understood me.
"I love you very much, and I know that you love me very much as well. Thank you for being such a wonderful father to me and for giving me so much love and support."
I think he was clinging to life mainly because he didn't want to leave my mother. Later, the second night, when it was just the two of them, my mother got in bed with my dad, held him, and felt him take his last breath. He was warm, felt safe, and knew he was loved and was finally able to "let go."
My father was one of the most important people in my life, and losing him was almost unendurable. The last year of his life, I spent part of almost every day with him. Even more than being my father, he was my "daddy," and no one ever has or ever will love me and support me as much as he did.

Once we finally arrive in Baltimore, more drama ensues while checking in. Either the handicapped room my mother booked and confirmed isn't available, or the rooms are too close to the elevator, or some other issue. The last time I tried to assist with this, while my father was still alive, I was told to "shut up." After that I did what I usually do in these situations. Stay out of the way, keep quiet, and use headphones! My brother and I usually share a room and, in the last few years, have been able to persuade my mother that these rooms did not need to have a connecting door. The last time we had a connecting door my brother, and I refused to unlock it, which ended up with my mother pounding on it and eventually going around to the door of our room and pounded on that until my brother opened it and got a tongue-lashing ending in both of us being uninvited to dinner. (I hid in the bathroom during this, so I didn't need to be part of this situation). This was another example of us bonding together like partners in crime. My mother seemed to feel that this connecting door should not only be unlocked but that she could come in and out of our room at her whim. We obviously did not agree.

My brother and I have been able to offer support and bond with one another during the time we are in Baltimore, watching several episodes of Law & Order SVU or movies that we both like and make us laugh, giving us much-needed comic relief. We make plans about schedules for bathroom time in the morning and listen to each other share one another's fears, worries, or thoughts about the upcoming appointments.

I told one of my best friends when I had recently been diagnosed that in a way, I was glad that I had the disease as well as my father and brother. I wasn't thinking about how they felt about being diagnosed, but I could only imagine the extent of survivor guilt I would have had if my brother had it and I didn't and how that would affect our family dynamic. Imagine the family dynamic that already existed with my mother having her three family members being diagnosed with this disease.

Family dynamics are challenging, and part of the damage that had been caused to my relationship with my brother had to do with the power differential in our family as well as the large differences in our own lives. I had always been cute, able to get away with a lot, and when necessary, fly under the radar. As I got older, I was very popular, and the friends that had previously been my brothers started to prefer my company as we became teenagers. This resulted in a lot of anger and jealousy. My brother struggled a lot more with the first symptoms of MD during adolescence than I did. The symptoms seemed to start affecting him earlier than they affected me. At around the time he was eight- or nine-years-old things in his life started going downhill, and this only continued.

Another aspect of our hospital day is escaping our parents for lunch since we are trying to make it through a very difficult day, which can be somewhat healed by junk food. My reasoning is that if I get a good report, I should be able to celebrate with my go-to comfort food, chicken fingers, and French fries. The flip side of this is if I don't get a good report, then I can use these same items to console myself.

The last year we went, the layout of the hospital, including the cafeteria, had changed drastically due to construction. My brother has a photographic memory and an innate sense of direction and was able to picture the hospital previously to determine where things were. This was a good thing since when we followed directions to the cafeteria, we found it was a new one, and the only options appeared to be healthy choices, which we had no interest in. We began a search to find the non-healthy cafeteria and ended up having to walk a long distance. While long distances are no picnic for me, especially in fancy shoes, they are doable; while in my brother's case, since his worst symptoms are a lack of mobility, it is much more difficult for him. He was able to recognize how much this meal meant to me, and he was able to persevere and direct us both to the cafeteria we were looking for, enabling us to get the meal we wanted.

My brother is one of the only people who responds to me being angry with him with a very calm, "you are only feeling that way because I won't do exactly what you want." His pointing this out only makes me angrier. As much as anyone, or maybe a slight bit more, I like to get my own way. I have often enjoyed having a great deal of success at this. However, my brother, whether he is just being contrary or really doesn't want to do what I am suggesting, is one of the only people who call me on this.

When talking recently with my mother about examples of times my brother and I bonded, she told me a story that I had no recollection of. When my brother was around eight or so, he started taking violin lessons. According to my mother, he really loved the violin but getting him to practice was a chore that she didn't feel like continuing. To this end, she told him that since he wouldn't practice, she was getting rid of his violin. His response to this apparently was to employ me to help him hide it. I don't have the slightest memory, but I do know that there were situations when my brother and I joined forces, as siblings often do, against our parents.

    Despite the struggles that I have in my relationship with my brother, as we get older and the emotional scars from our childhood heal or pass into less painful or distant memories, we can enjoy each other's company and get along as well as work toward common goals. I think part of this is because he knows that while my struggles are different than his, I do struggle. Also, I, more than anyone, understand how he feels.

DELAYED ADOLESCENCE

On these family trips, all sitting in one car together, I can't help but to reflect on my life and where I am, age 46, forced into the family dynamics of my adolescence due to my dependency on my family. I think about my mother at my same age, two teenagers in tow, independent of her own mother and not needing much help or support. MMD has lurched me into dependency on my mother, and we fall back to the familiar roles of my adolescence. In some ways, my mother has higher expectations for me than she has for my brother. Part of this is because I am currently much more physically and cognitively stronger, but also due to family dynamics. My brother and I joke about how I was my dad's favorite, and he is my mom's. (Our family dog, who recently passed away, was clearly my mother's favorite child). Although my parents denied this, there is evidence to the contrary.

Other times, my mother treats me the same way she does my brother. She is, especially currently, overly involved in all aspects of my life. I do not need to be reminded to eat breakfast or that I need more protein. I do not need help constructing emails. I am able to make good decisions about how I want to live my life, and I should be given the freedom and independence of someone in their 40s. I need the support, help, and love that my mother gives me, but being stuck in patterns that were established long ago no longer makes sense or is necessary.

INVISIBLE DISABILITY

Recently, a lady followed me out of the grocery store, came over to my car, and told me as if I hadn't noticed that I had parked in a handicapped spot. I had been distracted and forgotten to hang up my placard.

"Excuse me, young lady! Young lady!"

Walking toward my car after shopping at the co-op, I turned around to look at the elderly woman who was calling to me. She looked very agitated as she approached me and said: "You parked in a handicapped spot! These spots are for the people that need them, not for you!"

"I know I parked in a handicapped spot. I just forgot to hang up my placard."

"But you're not handicapped!"

Heaving a big sigh at this lady's ignorance, I decided I didn't have the energy to try and educate her.

"I'd be happy to show you my placard," I offered, trying to be polite.

As she continued to rail at me about how rude this was and how these spots were for people that really needed them, I took my placard out of the glove compartment and asked her if she would like to see it. She said she did not. "I didn't realize you're disabled. A lot of people your age are inconsiderate and park illegally in handicapped spaces." Apparently, it was her job to protect the handicapped spaces.

I would give people the benefit of the doubt, but this woman took it as her personal mission to make sure I was not stealing a parking space. She said, "You don't look disabled."

I don't feel like it is my job to educate people to the fact that judging someone by the way they look is like judging a book by its cover. Other people's ignorance is not my fault, and still, I have to pay for it.

An "invisible disability" is a disability that is not obvious to the casual observer and is often not noticed if it isn't mentioned. It is also a disability that others have an extremely hard time understanding. If someone doesn't know me or spend time with me it's likely they won't notice anything wrong or different about me. After all, to the casual observer, I appear "normal."

Everyone knows what it is like to feel tired, but pervasive fatigue is completely different and not very common. Having cataract surgery in your twenties and early 30s is rare and doesn't often happen. Using a handicap placard when you look totally normal can bring people to leave nasty notes on your car and follow you out of a store to give you a hard time.

MMD (and many other invisible disabilities) is hard to describe. You won't see anything out of the ordinary, at least not in the beginning. Even friends I have had before my onset don't really get it. And I hate being patronized. Having someone say "if you're too tired" or "if you feel up to it" makes me so mad. I will be the first to say if I am too tired and maybe I just don't feel like doing a certain activity. I live this way every single day, and I can determine what I can and cannot do. Sometimes I overestimate my abilities, but as time passes, I am better able to read myself. I like to be the one to make the decision of whether I can do anything.

My disability won't be invisible forever. At some time in the not-too-distant future, I will be seen as someone who is disabled. It is apparent when you see my brother that he is disabled. My disability is less obvious, hence the invisible part.

I am just like everyone else. I have good days and bad days, ups and downs, strengths and weaknesses. I am an average person and there is nothing about me that would stand out in a crowd. But I am unique, and I am my own person. I have troubles and successes, joy and sadness, sicknesses and health. And in this lifetime, I seem to encounter more sickness than health. It is not visible, and unless you know me well or I choose to share it with you, you would never know.

While I have this disability, I am not my diagnosis. It follows me around like the shell of a turtle because it is part of who I am, but is not what I am. I want to be the same as everyone else. There is so much judgment placed on people with disabilities, and I only want to be judged for my abilities and my intelligence, not how fast I can run a 50-yard dash or if I even can run a 50-yard dash.

Invisible Disability

My father and brother, who both have the same diagnosis have a visible disability. This is an example of pleiotropy, in which one gene influences many different traits. In my brother and father's case you can tell that they have a disability simply by observing them walk. In my case you could spend a day with me and not know that I have a disability.

People with "invisible" disabilities are discriminated against just as women, or minorities, or anyone in a group seen as "other." Those with "invisible" disabilities are discriminated against in another way since they are seen as having the ability to attend to all the details of a "normal" life, and when they cannot perform to this standard are seen as whining, lazy, or looking for attention or special treatment.

There is a medical model of disability which pertains to others being less willing to assist those with invisible disabilities because there is no outwardly apparent reason that this person needs assistance.

In the social model, there is discrimination in all the different facets of society. In the workplace, if someone applied for a job that had vision or speech impairment and was qualified for the job, accommodations would be put in place to assist them, and every effort would be made to cause them not to be discriminated against. The Americans with Disabilities Act mandates this. However, someone with pervasive fatigue may not want to disclose this for fear of not being offered a job or employment. Even though I am fatigued, I have no trouble staying awake but on certain days, attending work is a significant challenge.

I remember reading that it is estimated that 96% of people with chronic medical conditions live with an illness that is invisible. It is also estimated that 10% of the people in the US have a medical condition that may be considered an invisible disability, and nearly one out of two people in the US have a chronic medical condition that doesn't impact or impair their daily functioning.

When I am either trying to explain what my daily life is like to other people or explain why I can't or am unable to do something, it is often met with exasperated expressions or seen as an excuse or trying to get out of doing my fair share of work.

Situations such as attending an all-day conference that is over an hour's drive each way are an example. I will go if it is mandatory, but this makes for an incredibly exhausting long day for me and becomes almost impossible if I must do the transportation. Whether or not I want to attend the conference is not the point, but if I mention that I would rather not go, I am seen as not being a team member or trying to shirk my duties.

Last time this came up, I was told everyone else has had to go, and I need to pay my dues. In this case, I was able to make my own accommodations, get a ride from a coworker, and take the next day off.

Another example is moving furniture in a room to prepare for an activity. I am more than willing to help, but moving chairs, long tables, or rugs is much more difficult for me than an able-bodied person. The fact that I look able-bodied causes it to appear that I am slacking. I am so willing to always give everyone the benefit of the doubt. I have found this to be a unique quality because for me getting the benefit of the doubt, even with those who know my diagnosis, is not guaranteed.

TAKE FAIR OUT OF THE DICTIONARY

After more than 40 years on this earth, I know that for me fair doesn't exist. Life isn't fair, and expecting it to be is an exercise in futility. Most of life isn't fair, either in a positive or negative way. It's not fair that some people have more than they could ever use, and others have none. There is the luck of the draw and random circumstances, but very little can be deemed fair. Having MMD is especially not fair.

As I lay in bed, trying to summon the will to get up, I have two divergent factions running through my mind. One is the desire to live each day to the fullest, participate in society, and enjoy every moment; the desire to do my best to live in the present, the here and now. The other faction is the vision of long, endless years, every day of my life taking enormous effort to get through and no end in sight; the futility of trying to find the energy to push, plod, and power through just one more day or at least go through the motions. This vision leaves me totally depressed and more than a little frightened. It is the fear that I will wake up tomorrow and be 60, with my whole life having passed me by, with nothing to look forward to and nothing in my past but failure.

I have learned a lot by observing, through my own life, what it is like to live with the symptoms of an incurable, debilitating disease. The physical effects are challenging enough, but as I strive to relate my life and dreams to a different body and lifestyle than the one I always imagined, I find the emotional effects at the forefront of my daily struggles.

There are so many questions about the direction my disability is forcing me to go, including new questions and thoughts that I would never have entertained otherwise. Where do I make the effort, and where to give myself a break? How to live my life to the fullest when I am stuck between wanting to spend quality time with my husband and the almost overwhelming desire to retreat to bed and not emerge again. I see myself coming home, and the image I have is of a hurt animal hurrying into its burrow, whimpering as it goes, searching for safety, comfort and respite.

How do I rectify the life I am living with the life I wanted. How do I continue every day as I watch my dreams painfully fade. I am a stable, intelligent, adult but do not have the ability to make some of the most important decisions about my own life. I exist in a place where the door that leads to emptiness and oblivion looks pretty good. On many days I live the statement of not wanting to live and not wanting to die, but I can't bear to exist in the shadowed middle world between the two.

There is also the struggle that exists between my limitations and my intense amount of determination. Quite often this gets me into trouble by biting off more than I can chew. Whenever someone tells me I can't do something I have an overwhelming need to prove them wrong. I will work so hard to convince others that I can do something that I end up convincing myself in the process, even if the action or activity that I am trying to prove I can do is something totally out of my reach. While I have made the decision to avoid activities that are going to be way too much for me as well as giving myself the option of taking a break, this often causes me to feel like a loser. I have a sort of "pull yourself up by the bootstraps" or "get over yourself" mentality.

There have been people in my life who considered me to just be lazy or felt that I could do it if I really wanted to. There were also many years when I was experiencing symptoms with no diagnosis, and the constant frustration of not being able to do things that I had easily done before caused immense feelings of failure.

This isn't about the past. This is about what comes after the diagnosis and the realization that you have a disease and the ramifications of that. This is not about how angry I am and how this is not fair, and all the other emotions that have emerged. This is about me finding my voice, finding a vehicle to work through my own emotions, and in some way, make a difference to someone. This is about me saying I have something to share and giving myself the opportunity to speak while I can, for whatever that is worth. This is my chance to make sense of my changed life and discover a way to define myself, and go forward from the dark and damaging place of loss and longing. No, it's not fair. But in order to be successful, I must let that go.

My goal, in the end, is to find the willingness and ability to let go and to be who I am meant to be.

MAYBE YOU'RE JUST LAZY

The word lazy is defined as unwillingness to work or use energy, lack of effort, or activity. Since I exert all my energy, am willing and expend a great deal of effort in most areas of my life I would say I am decidedly un-lazy. I wouldn't say that I was the opposite of lazy, which is energetic, but I become outraged when people accuse me of being lazy.

You could do it if you really wanted to. This is one of my favorite expressions. Have I mentioned that I'm sarcastic? This indicates a lack of determination or selfishness on my part, neither of which I have ever been accused of having. Just because I want to do something doesn't mean I can or will be able to. If that were the case, I would be out doing whatever I wanted right now.

If you rest all day, you can do an evening activity tonight. This suggests that you can store up energy to use when needed. This is great in theory, but sadly not an actuality. If I could store energy, I would be a much more energetic person. I could rest until the cows come home and still not have an ounce of the energy necessary to do anything. On the other hand, I could not rest at all and be ready for an activity.

I no longer drive home after extreme exercise because I am so tired, I am afraid to. Whenever I go somewhere with my husband, family, or friends, they often drive, not because I can't, but it really tires me out. Having to concentrate or focus for long periods of time often leads me to be completely depleted. I have noticed lately that when I over-exercise or completely deplete the very limited resources I have, it causes me to almost hallucinate.

However, there were days when I would go snowboarding or skiing and then come home to shower and go out with friends. You never really know how tired you will be or when you could go no longer. Granted, I am tired ALL THE TIME. This is a constant in an ever-changing world. I often quantify my level of tiredness because it does not suffice just to say that I am tired.

Can't you just power through? With just a little more effort on my part, it is thought that I can get through anything. Unfortunately, even when I desperately want to power through, there is no guarantee that I will be able to.

A friend picked me up at the airport when I was returning from a vacation with aspiration pneumonia. I had spent most of the day traveling and was totally done in. When I had arrived at the airport that morning and was going through security, I realized I was at Terminal A, and I needed to get to terminal D. When the TSA agent told me how far it was, I literally got tears in my eyes. There was no other option than to do whatever I had to. I told my friend that even though I had the next day off from work, I was dreading the day after. She asked me, "Can't you just power through?" I would have laughed if I hadn't felt so dreadful. I had used all my resources and then some, and there was no power left to power through anything.

Maybe you're just lazy. I would love the opportunity to be lazy and see what that feels like. I never really have the opportunity to just be lazy. This does not mean that there aren't days when I only do the bare minimum or days I don't get dressed or leave the house. But to have the choice to be lazy or not would be a great luxury. To actually revel in my laziness and answer "maybe you're just lazy" with "Yup. I guess I am."

PART FIVE

SINGLES

SINGLES

I went to CA to spend New Year's 2002 with my friend Kelly. One of the days we were together we decided to play tennis. We went to the courts and hit the ball around for a while. Kelly had taken lessons and enjoyed playing, and of course, I took any opportunity to play. Eventually, we talked about what we wanted to do.

"We can play the game to 21 points or work on different shots or whatever you want."

"I want to play for real."

"You'll hit a lot more balls if we just hit back and forth."

"I want to play a match!"

"Why?"

"I want to win a game off you."

"Kelly, that's not going to happen."

In tennis, the game of singles is between two opponents, one on each side of the net. It doesn't matter if you are playing for fun, as part of a league or team, or professionally; when you are playing singles, you are on your own. You can't depend on another teammate, tap out or trade places. It is only you, your racket, and your skills against an opponent.

If you are just playing for fun, and there aren't any stakes involved, any sense of anxiety is greatly reduced. When you are a fierce competitor like me, there are always stakes involved, even if only in your own head. Singles is my favorite form of tennis and the one I play most often. While I train and compete in doubles, I am more comfortable playing singles. There is a difference in the skills and shots used in singles versus doubles and a different strategy. I do enjoy having a partner to depend on and interact with and often have a lot of fun in my doubles matches, but singles are where my real passion lies.

In essence, every part of your game, your strengths and weaknesses, movement ability, and shot selection are the only tools you have in your arsenal. Whether you are allowed coaching or not, the only person playing the match (other than your opponent) is you. While all the different components of your game are important, one of the most important parts is your inner monologue: your ability to either promote yourself or diminish yourself in the thoughts and scenarios running through your head.

There are days when you just can't play to the level that you usually do. The weather, heat, sun, wind, court conditions, and even time and spectators are all elements that you have to battle and adjust to. If you are tired, or injured, or just having a bad day, your general outlook and, thereby, your match play will be greatly affected. There is your opponent's attitude and spectators that can be disruptive. If you are focusing on any of these distractions, your mind will not be where it needs to be for you to be successful.

One of the aspects of matches that commentators generally give a lot of importance to is the mental game of different players. A coach who used to play my mother told me that she had given my mother the advice that you should never know what your opponent is wearing during a match. Basically, she was saying your focus should be totally on yourself. She was lamenting the fact that ever since she had told my mother this, she had never won another set off her.

Some players have more tendency than others to get down on themselves, and their match is negatively impacted. It can also be used to get yourself psyched up. Others play better when they are losing or down in the score count. It is sometimes easy to see who the most experienced player in a match is, not necessarily because they are the better player, but because they can take a negative (or positive) situation and change it. An example is being down a set or losing a set badly and being able to come back and win the match. Another part of this is closing out a match. When you are winning and getting close to the end of the match, there is the tendency to get "tight" or lose focus and end up not being able to finish the match. Tenacity is very important, and it is imperative not to lose sight of your overall goal.

When I first started playing wheelchair tennis, I wasn't overly concerned about winning or losing my competition matches. I was more focused on whether I had moved, how well I had moved, and tried to correct as many of the mistakes I made as well as I could. This, as well as training, was the only way I will continue to improve.

I am very competitive, and I like to win. As predicted, despite my developing MMD, I won the match against Kelly 6-0. At 26, I was already experiencing rough fatigue symptoms, and it took me over a day to recover, but we had a great time. I still use all my matches as learning experiences and do my best to not get down on myself when I lose a match badly. I use mental focus and positive self-talk to encourage myself. I have played matches against opponents who have played in a wheelchair for 25 years or who play several times a week, or are permanently in a wheelchair, meaning they have much more control and movement ability.

All I can do is my best; use all the skills and tools I have and play as well as I possibly can.

ALONE

At the time in my life when I was diagnosed, I had no capacity for being alone. I didn't dread anything as much as being alone with myself. The minute that loneliness began to loom, I was on the phone or heading out the door. Nothing was worse than being by myself. I have spent most of my life in one relationship or another since seventh grade. These relationships were frequently changed, occasionally overlapped; some were serious, some casual, and I did anything necessary to not have to be in my own head. This makes it possible to completely avoid any loneliness or soul searching of any sort.

I have often noticed that the periods of time when I was drawn to journaling and being contemplative were the times in my life when I was single or going through a sea change. In order to make sense of my life, the changes, and struggles, I needed to gain the clarity that is achieved by setting it all down in writing. Having my thoughts all in a jumble makes it impossible to concentrate on any one thought, feeling, emotion, or idea. By putting it down on paper, it forces me to be coherent, thus making it easier to examine. When I was in a relationship, I focused on that rather than myself, and that made it difficult to have any introspection apart from the details and drives of my current entanglement.

Relationships of all kinds are vital in our lives. Some are good, some are bad, and each one is different and affects us in a different way. In romantic relationships, it is often easy to lose yourself in the glow of love and fusion that occurs. While being involved can bring relief and be relieving, for a variety of reasons, it can keep you out of your head and your own thoughts. I have had many relationships that were positive, and that helped me to define and understand myself, but I have had just as many that limited me and caused me to doubt myself. Being my own person, thinking my own thoughts that are not dictated or directed by others, is the most important part of becoming an individual.

"We seem so frightened today of being alone that we never let it happen," says Anne Lindbergh. "We must re-learn to be alone." (Lindbergh, 41, 42). She includes that it is most important for women. I needed to learn the art of being alone, but without the result being loneliness. To view being alone as a positive and to find a way to enjoy and revel in my own space and time without feeling lonely. The art of being comfortable in my own skin requires an ability to face my thoughts and emotions. This can be a very frightening proposition, especially when the situation of being alone with my thoughts has been avoided. No matter what the alternative may be, it is better than being alone. How many people enter or remain in a relationship for the sole purpose of not having to be alone? Not just to have someone to celebrate major holidays with or a built-in partner for the movies or to go out to eat with, but just to fend off having to be in a space by yourself. What does it say about us, that we would rather spend time with someone we may not even like than face the possibility of having no one around? I think loneliness is one of the most common emotions that people try to escape from.

How much time does one ever actively or voluntarily spend alone? Depending on your situation, it can be a lot or a little. I have always needed alone time, but forced loneliness or being by myself when it isn't my own choice was very difficult. That is a challenge that I have only begun to be comfortable with in the last few years. While married, I knew that my period of being alone had firm parameters.

When I lived alone in a studio in Colorado, I would go shopping just to be around people. I would go to the neighborhood bar and grill just to have contact with others. I wanted to have the sensation of people around me but not necessarily need to interact. Although challenging, this was a real period of growth, and I gained an incredible amount of resilience from this. I hardly knew anyone, was far away from my family, and in an unknown area. I gained a lot of skills in being alone, including insight and introspection.

Not being in a relationship or having the constant distraction of someone around me day and night opened the door for me to inspect my life and my circumstances to determine where I was at this present moment and where I wanted to be at any moment in the future. I spent most of my first few months in Denver outside, in the sun, writing in my journal and trying to determine how I could make my life work in its present incantation. I was able to inspect my life without fear; I was able to learn a great deal about myself and see the patterns, both positive and negative, that I had engaged in.

Once I entered back into a relationship, I ceased journaling and again allowed a relationship to dictate my life. Having partners who previously didn't have acceptance of themselves can be scary as it leads to the belief that once they have found this acceptance, they will no longer need us. In secure, mature relationships, we can guide and support others in finding acceptance and realize that it will not lead them to stop needing us, rather, it will allow them to need us in a different way.

As soon as my last relationship prior to meeting my husband ended, I began journaling again to try and understand why I couldn't seem to escape this particular relationship. I was amazed to come to the realization that I was finally done with this cycle. For me, it was over, and I could end this toxic situation. Despite the daunting prospect of being alone, that was better than being in a relationship that was only hurting and causing me pain. Worst of all, it was causing me to lose and constantly second-guess myself, which was eroding any self-confidence I had and any belief in my worth as a person. I have had enough struggles and doubts on my own to have another person add to them. Especially someone who was supposed to be loving toward me and supporting me.

I was moving towards acceptance of myself in all areas, but especially as a woman dealing with a difficult disease. This acceptance was so hard won I didn't want there to be anyone trying to undermine my progress or process. It made it much harder to gain acceptance of myself while being in a relationship with someone who was, under the guise of helping me grow to my potential, causing me to go in the other direction.

The spring this relationship ended, I was finally able to escape a situation that had been in control of me for four years, and to begin again to explore my life and myself. I enjoyed every moment of being alone. I had dealt with the demons of loneliness before and was now able to revel in my space and time, the ability to do my own thing and to continue my personal development. Without the distraction of a relationship, I was totally focused on myself and loved every minute of it.

Anne Morrow Lindbergh talks about home and everyday life, which is filled with distractions and leaves very little time for self or contemplation. To me, this is the same as all-consuming relationships, which also leave little time for contemplation. I experience a need for quiet time, to think, be by myself and remove myself from the distractions and stress of everyday life.

One needs time to listen to what your creative spirit is trying to tell you and what you can hear if you are able to silence all the chaos around you and listen to your inner being, which speaks the truth and is the essence of who you are.

The art of being alone is what I began to learn while at the Gonzaga and Omega retreats and when I first lived on my own in Colorado. The lessons took a long time to germinate, but I ended up enjoying my own company and my solitude so much that I started to need to have it every day.

Finding the true essence of yourself is one of those hard-won talents. As children, we are on the surface; our every thought, idea, feeling, and emotion is out there for everyone to see. We have little artifice and lack the protective camouflage that we begin to develop as soon as possible. Without feeling these emotions and going through this process, it is impossible to find the true essence of you.

The lessons I began learning were used to start to cope with my diagnosis. They took many years to take root and are still issues that I struggle with daily. Coming to terms with my diagnosis and the changes it presents in my life is a process I will never be done with. Continuing to learn these lessons is what makes it possible for me to find ways to live with such a disease. The challenges never become easier; they just change.

The irony of this, of course, is that now, having learned that being alone is important and has become something I crave, I have less opportunity to be alone due to becoming progressively more dependent on having people around to help support me.

Alone

The MSW program gave me a new frame of reference for using writing as a tool and for doing work that resonated with my situation and myself. Writing for myself and for school was a way to start to understand a new way of living that was different from what I had presumed would be my life, which was now lying in tatters at my feet. I didn't know how, and I didn't know what, but I knew there was something that I was meant to do, and I needed to discover what that was.

MY PLACE

During the summer, I loved the mornings when my father would say, "It looks like a beach day." Hearing this would fill me with a sense of complete joy. Joy that there is such a thing as a "beach day" with all that implies to me and that I am in the perfect place to enjoy it to the fullest.

The beach has always been "my place." No matter what my struggle is, when I can get to the beach, I always feel better. It can be in the summer, lying on the beach, and absorbing the combination of sun, sand, sea, and salt air. It can be on gray, rainy, or cold days. Even in the colder months, with the watery sun and the wind whipping, the beach can still be my refuge. I can have perfect moments, perfect hours, and perfect days on the beach when they are so difficult to come by in other places. It takes only me to have a perfect moment or perfect hour, and other people usually accompany perfect days. It is easy to find perfection in so many dimensions of the beach. Having a perfect moment, or hour, or day can lead us to more solace.

Whether it is walking on the beach, looking at the water, or hearing the waves, this is where I am most happy and tranquil. Anne Lindberg's words appeal to me: "Beauty of the earth and sea and air meant more to me. I was in harmony with it, melted into the universe, lost in it..." (Lindbergh 43).

I can be in harmony with my universe and myself when I have the sand between my toes, the sun on my face, and the vast emptiness of the ocean before me. The beach is a feeling for me, a state of mind, as much as a place. All my senses are involved, including smell. When I press my face into my beach towel, I can smell the essence of the beach and can be transported in my mind. To most, the towel smells like it simply needs to be washed, but to me, it embodies the smell of summer and all the elements of the beach. I have a sign hanging in my kitchen, "Sun, sand, & salty air." That says it all.

Lindbergh talks about bringing shells from the beach back to her desk to help her to "...keep my core, my center, my island quality." (Lindbergh 58) I have a shell that is on my desk and one I wear around my neck to remind me there is a place I can go to find my center and my core and escape from all the distractions of life. It is where I can regain my equilibrium and a sense of balance.

I have a collection of sand from my favorite beaches. Just seeing the sand can bring happy feelings and the image that I can literally carry the beach with me wherever I go.

The beach has been a big part of my life since I was born. Growing up, I spent most or all the summer by the beach. It is one of my favorite memories of childhood and even thinking of it now warms me. Whenever life was particularly challenging for me, I knew going to the beach would be healing and help me to find perspective.

When I found myself in the hospital for the fourth time within a one-and-a-half-year span, I knew I needed a break. The only place I wanted to be was the beach. As I got stronger, I was able to walk on the beach, which I love. For many weeks, I spent part of every day on the beach, sitting, laying down, reading, looking out to sea, thinking, and just being. I love to have sand on my feet and enjoy even the feeling of having sand between my toes in my bed.

The beach feeds my soul, even in the worst of times. This has been my mantra about the beach for many years when trying to explain its importance. It is the times that I can go to the beach and just "be" that calms my mind, soothes my soul, and takes me away from all the distractions, stress, hustle, and drama that infuses each day. "The problem is more how to still the soul in the midst of its activities. In fact, the problem is how to feed the soul." (Lindbergh 51).

Feeding my soul and stilling it from its frantic pace is of utmost importance to me. In my mind, my soul is the essence of who I am and is at the very core of my being. Starving my soul is the same to me as starving my body. Since it is not food but rather other intangible things that feed my soul, I must do all I can to be vigilant and keep my soul fed.

The beach also brings me balance. There is a rhythm to the beach, the waves, the tide, and the different seasons as seen on the shore. The peace and grace that I feel at the beach is something I don't feel anywhere else.

My Place

I love the concept of simplicity. The basic premise that simple is good applies to all aspects of life. It is the simple things that matter the most and the simple things that bring harmony between our inner and outer selves. It is places such as the beach that can lead us to simplicity so that we might create this spiritual connection in ourselves.

I want to emphasize that a place can be a feeling as well as a certain state of mind. I have a beach state of mind. I bring the beach with me, through shells, bottles of sand, jars of sea glass, and the belief that the beach will be there for me whenever I need it.

BEING THANKFUL

Giving thanks and being thankful leads to peace and joy. It is possible to look at each day and find small parts of life to give thanks for. It is the ability to see positives in every situation, to find possibilities or a silver lining. While it can be very easy to not feel thankful for anything during our daily lives, every day, we must look at our lives and realize what we have to be thankful for. I am often thankful for things that I had, even if they are now lost. I am thankful that I had them and optimistic that I may have them again. When bitterness that I lost them threatens to loom, I do my best to turn it around. Like the cliché that it is better to have loved and lost than never to have loved at all.

I am thankful for things long past, things I did for myself, and things others did for me. Every day I try to think of things I am grateful for and to not take anything for granted as I have learned that nothing is certain.

It is the simple things, seeing the sunshine, feeling the breeze in my hair, the smell of the beach and the ocean, and the time to do the things that I love. Despite all the negatives I experience, these are what make me thankful, perhaps more thankful than I would be had I not lost anything or had not lost as much as I have.

Gratitude or being grateful and thankful are, to me, two sides of the same coin. I can be grateful and thankful for the same things, but I consider them to be separate. While I am grateful for the health I have, I am not grateful for the struggles I have with my health. However, I am thankful that I have some resources to deal with my health struggles. I must continue creating and cultivating gratitude. Otherwise, I will end up alone and bitter. I must find and direct this gratitude to myself, which in turn is being thankful for me. Gratitude that I have this body, with all its faults and frailties, rather than someone different. Gratitude that I have this life to live, despite all the pain and suffering I endure. Gratitude for my thoughts, dreams, wishes, and desires.

"You were given life; it is your duty (and also your entitlement as a human being) to find something beautiful within life, no matter how slight." (Gilbert 115)

I intend to do all I can before I leave this earth. There is a reason I was born, a reason that I am afflicted with this disability, and my deep desire to help others. My strongest goal is to make something beautiful of this life and to use all the passion and strength I have in order to leave something powerful behind.

PART SIX

TWO BOUNCES

TWO BOUNCES

Wheelchair tennis changed my world and saved my life. If I hadn't found wheelchair tennis, I don't know where I'd be today. The opportunity to travel, compete, and train in an activity I'm passionate about has made all the difference for me. For years, I missed and mourned the absence of tennis. The fact that I'd had to give up something that had been such a huge part of my life was demoralizing and painful.

By 2017, I'd reached a point where I realized that the only way I was going to be able to continue playing tennis was in a wheelchair. I hadn't played for a few years since playing for even just 15 minutes completely exhausted me. Because my weight had totally transferred onto my heels, it was impossible for me to run, jump, bounce, or even move very quickly. If you play tennis, then you know what I'm talking about: firmly planted feet are death in this game. Being a good tennis player requires literally being on your toes, something that I could no longer do. Whereas before, every move had been fluid, I now felt awkward and off balance.

The format and rules are almost the same as able-bodied tennis, and any training or instruction is helpful. But the better I get at wheelchair tennis, the more I understand that it is a completely different game. The biggest difference in the rules between able-bodied tennis and wheelchair tennis is that in wheelchair tennis, you are allowed two bounces to return the ball rather than just one. This gives you more time to get to the ball because wheelchairs move slower than feet. The faster you return the ball, the less time your opponent has to get set up to return, which is great. But the faster you return the ball, the faster it comes back to you. Having two bounces, as I quickly figured out, can be very useful.

That said, getting used to two bounces is difficult in terms of timing. In a wheelchair, you're much lower to the ground, which is already quite an adjustment as it requires moving in such a way that the ball doesn't bounce over your head. In my first competitive match, I lost a lot of points this way. In able-bodied tennis, one of your main objectives is to move forward. But charging ahead in a wheelchair can cause the ball to bounce right over you. In that case, having two bounces doesn't help in the least.

I tried several different wheelchairs and a variety of equipment in order to determine what works the best for me. Initially, I used an old racket, figuring that any would do. I quickly learned that weight and grip size are significant factors in a racket to be compatible with wheelchair tennis. The racket was quite heavy and had a large grip size for my hand, which would have been challenging on its own. Adding a wheelchair, I was sunk. I had trouble holding the racket, especially when trying to wheel, and if I could hang on to the racket at all, it often flew out of my hand when I made contact with the ball or even if I just took a swing.

Occasionally, I just dropped it. Other times, the racket would go flying across the court, which was dangerous for bystanders, not to mention making winning any points impossible for me. I couldn't keep a firm grip while serving, and any attempt at power was dismal. I ended up wearing gloves and had the handle of the racket sanded down to make it easier to grip. I also added a wrist strap to keep the racket from flying out of my hand.

Michaela, who I played against in my first tournament, used this high, arcing shot constantly. Since I was not yet skilled in wheelchair tennis and was still using the instincts from able-bodied tennis, I moved forward again and again as Michaela's shots arched above me. Over time I'd learned to hit this shot quite well myself, but in those first attempts, it was incredibly frustrating.

Just like in able-bodied tennis, the area between the baseline and the service line is called "no man's land," and it's a place you don't want to be. I try to stay behind the baseline to avoid no man's land, but it's tough since a lot of balls bounce around the service line. This was another big adjustment for me. Wheelchair tennis players hit the ball far less hard than their able-bodied counterparts.

I started out convinced that since I was an accomplished tennis player, adapting to playing on wheels would be no trouble. This has not been the case. When I have trouble reaching the ball in time, I remember that I have two bounces. While that can help when I'm trying to reach a drop shot or a short ball, the extra bounce doesn't always help. Sometimes the second bounce ends up being behind me, in which case I still can't get to it. Letting the ball bounce again can also end up making it even further away than it was after the first bounce.

I've come to think of those two bounces as a metaphor. In life, you occasionally need two bounces to get into a better position, to have enough time to prepare, or to move so that you can pull off a stronger shot rather than relying on a weaker one. When things are going well in life, you only need one bounce, but sometimes it is very helpful to have two.

I have realized that at this point in my life, I now need two bounces. In most areas of my life, more effort is required to accomplish anything, even things that I didn't give a second thought to in the past. Some things are insurmountable, no matter how many bounces I have.

This is just one more of the many things I have had to accept, such as my inevitable acceptance that I could no longer play able-bodied tennis. I must combat the anger and depression that accompanies each change until I am able to reach acceptance. My years of winning at every sport I tried meant I never needed to learn how to accept defeat. It has been an incredibly hard journey to go from a fiercely competitive athlete to less than that.

I have been able to find avenues around the roadblocks. Wheelchair tennis is an example. I do suffer jealousy and flashes of anger at times. Luckily, I am still able to do something I love, just modified.

At times, two bounces make life more challenging. If the second bounce is behind you, or moves the ball further away from you, it is of no use. If you can't get the ball on one bounce, you have to forfeit the point. When I think about activities that I can no longer achieve or must structure my life in a new way, I can use the memories of all the times I did these certain activities or times when I didn't need structure of any sort. If I need two bounces now, then I thank my lucky stars that two bounces are allowed.

HELPING HAND

My mother has an amazing gift of finding people to help her in a variety of areas. Since she is usually willing to help others, if she can, others are willing to help her. There are so many people who are always asking what they can do to help and letting her know they are only a phone call away if she needs anything.

A recent example of this is when my mom had surgery. My brother and I had lists with several people on them to call with updates and news. Other friends and family members also had lists. Everyone has family and friends, but the sheer number of them far exceeded the usual amount of people waiting in the wings. My mother comes from a very large, close-knit family, so there were a lot of relatives, but the same number, if not even more, of friends.

Another example is when I lost my cell phone at a rest stop in New York. I didn't realize I'd lost it until I got home. Luckily, it was found, but it had to be picked up two hours away. My mother was able to find someone to drive down and get it. One year, when my aunt from California was visiting us in Vermont in the winter, and her flight was rerouted to New Hampshire, my mom found someone to pick her up the next day, three hours away. These are the kind of things that you can't just ask anyone to do. She repays this help and these kindnesses, and it is a two-way street, but it is amazing to have these kinds of connections. A lot of these people have ended up being invaluable.

My mother also has a lot of connections through tennis. Tennis has been a huge part of her life, and if you're looking for my mother, chances are she is on a court somewhere. She has a large network of friends and acquaintances that she plays with that continues to widen.

Her tennis connections have also become part of the helping hand. For instance, my mom plays tennis with Jennifer, my amazing editor. This connection changed my life. She instilled me with confidence that my story is worth telling.

Another example is when my husband and I were buying a condo, both the listing agent and the selling agent had played tennis with my mother. An early tennis partner of my mother's even became my godmother! It is through my mother's tennis connections that I was able to find several "angels" that have been invaluable to me.

One of the angels in my life is Michael Mercier. I was desperately looking for someone to coach me in wheelchair tennis and hadn't had any luck. Someone my mom knew through tennis recommended him.

Michael is an accomplished player and coach and has been very involved in wheelchair tennis. In the summer of 2017, I met with him several times for lessons and instruction. He was the force behind my ability to play wheelchair tennis to any degree of success. He realized my fierce competitive nature and was able to help me use it to my advantage. Wheelchair tennis is such a challenging sport that if you don't have a strong desire to learn, you aren't going to get very far and will quickly give up in defeat.

At our first meeting, he loaned me a much better chair than the one I had rented, and got rid of my wrist strap, gloves, and my altered, ineffective, outdated, heavy racket. He gave me a lightweight racket with a smaller handle than the one I was using and got me moving.

In the first year or two that I played, I tried several different gloves to protect my hands and improve my grip on the racket handle. I had racquetball, football, cycling, and any other sports glove I could find to help me hang onto my racket. Even with the lightweight racket, it was constantly flying out of my hand or being dropped. I used a rubber band to keep the racket attached to my hand, which worked with varying success. Although I still lost my grip, it didn't go flying.

Michael and I met several times over the summer and early fall. I eventually found this to be fun and quite a workout. He was always supportive and willing to help and taught me many of the ins and outs of wheelchair tennis. We have been able to meet a few times in the last couple of years, and I continue to value him greatly as a coach and mentor.

There are so many components and strategies to wheelchair tennis that are completely absent in able-bodied people. Without this instruction, I would still be playing able-bodied tennis, albeit in a wheelchair. This would lead me to struggle even more than I already do.

Michael also got me involved in the wheelchair tennis community, without which I would have had no way to form the connections I made. Toward the end of the summer of 2017, Michael invited me to Newport, where there was a wheelchair tennis player being inducted into the Tennis Hall of Fame. She gave a short speech about her experience as a top-level wheelchair tennis player that was very interesting and informative. She added that if you are just going to play on the local courts with friends for fun and aren't going to be competing that your equipment isn't very important. However, if you were planning on competing, you needed to have top-of-the-line equipment. This was reinforced later that afternoon when one of my borrowed wheelchair tires exploded, which made a sound like a gunshot and scared me almost to death. At first, I didn't know what had happened, but many of the others did. It was a very hot day, and the courts were so hot that my tire had overheated.

I also got my first taste of judgment, which I had not expected. I figured that there was a somewhat level playing field since we were all in wheelchairs, whatever our disability may be. This is not the case. Since I could no longer play after my tire exploded, I got up out of my chair and was immediately told by another player that I was cheating because I could walk. I was so startled and so tired, sunburned, and overwhelmed that I decided to call it a day. That was the first experience I had with someone thinking that since I wasn't in a wheelchair full time, I shouldn't be able to use one to play in. I have been questioned or given a hard time occasionally by other players who think that being able to walk gives me an advantage. Being able to walk is certainly an advantage in life but is immaterial in wheelchair tennis.

There is also often speculation about people claiming that they are more disabled or that their disability is more restrictive than it really is. The only reason I can see for doing this is to be able to play in the quadriplegic division rather than having to play against others who may not be as impacted as you, therefore giving them an advantage. I cannot imagine someone who is willing to make their disability seem worse than it is just for a small advantage and perhaps a greater chance of winning.

Even though it had been exhausting, I had immensely enjoyed the afternoon. The experience I had of being with other players, hitting some balls, fooling around, and feeling like part of a new group was exhilarating.

At tournaments, I had seen several players who taped the racket to their hands. Obviously, that was a much better way to control it, but it was not a step I was yet willing to take.

Eventually, I was introduced to a wheelchair player who taped the racket to his hand. He was willing to wrap my hand and hit a few balls just to see how I liked it. It was an amazing revelation. I had so much more control that any drawbacks were sure to be minimal in comparison to how much I gained. Usually, players who tape the racket to their hands are unable to play any other way. I did need to figure out how to hit the ball hard without losing my grip on the racket.

He made a video of his hand being taped and sent it to me so I could have a template. Since then, I have been taping my hand. It takes a lot of adjustments and tinkering to get it right, and I have had to learn how to move my chair with a racket taped to my hand, but it makes it possible for me to hit the ball hard and serve with some power. The freedom and the knowledge that I wasn't going to either lose my racket or decapitate someone with it had been immense.

Initially, I used his technique of wrapping the racket handle with tape, sticky side up, and after securing his hand to the racket, wrapping the outside. Since my main problem is my grip strength and not my hands, I don't have to be quite so intense. This has made a huge difference in my ability and comfort level. I occasionally whack myself with the connected racket, and for the time I am playing, I only have one available hand. I do long for the days when all I needed to do was lace up my sneakers, grab a racket and go. The amount of gear is extensive, and taping my hand is time consuming and requires another person.

Another "angel" who has been invaluable in assisting me in wheelchair tennis is Greg Hasterok from California. Several years ago, my mother had been playing and noticed Greg playing wheelchair tennis on the next court. She introduced herself and told him about my interest in the sport. My mom had tried to set me up to train with Greg since I've been playing, but he had always been competing in Europe when I was in California.

I went out to CA in late February 2019 to train for the upcoming 2019 Cajun Classic. My mom had contacted Greg, and he was willing to work with me while I was out there. We set a time to meet at the local courts. I was nervous, but he immediately put me at ease. He was very friendly, and I found it fun, very informative, and extremely helpful.

We worked on different parts of my game, and it was the first time I had private lessons from someone who not only knew but played wheelchair tennis. Before Greg had the accident that put him in a wheelchair, he had never played tennis before. He had the benefit of learning to play when he was already in a wheelchair. It's a big transition from playing able-bodied tennis to playing in a wheelchair and it's easier to learn the game if you already have the chair movement skills. A bonus to this is that you don't have to correct any old habits you picked up from playing able-bodied.

Many wheelchair players use an inverted backhand, which gives them more power and control. Instead of hitting the ball with the back of your hand facing the net, they invert their hand, so it's like a cross-body forehand. I tried several times to learn this shot with little success. My backhand has suffered since I went from a two-handed to a one-handed backhand, and since my hand is now taped to my racket, I am unable to change my grip from a forehand to a backhand. Not only is my backhand weaker, but my wrist is weaker, causing my racket to give when it contacts the ball. This usually results in either the ball going into the net or being a high lob. Since neither of these is the shot I'm trying to execute, it is not very effective.

LEARNING THE BASICS

There were several people and places involved in my introduction and training in wheelchair tennis. From the first time I ever saw a wheelchair to now, when I am competing in several tournaments a year, I wouldn't have gotten half as far without those who have been willing to help and guide me.

In the spring of 2017, when I visited my mother in California, she told me that she had talked to the pro at Balboa Park, where she played. He had found a sport wheelchair I could borrow and was willing to give me a basic introductory wheelchair tennis lesson. I had never been in or even seen a sport wheelchair in real life but was excited. Before the first lesson, I was able to try sitting in the chair.

Wheelchairs, in general, have changed a lot and are much smaller, especially those that are designed to be self-propelled.

Sport wheelchairs are like these new wheelchairs except that their wheels are very canted, which makes it possible to execute tight turns and the ability to switch direction and maneuver. They also have three small wheels on the bottom frame, one that extends in the back and two on either side in the front. These are stabilizers to help keep your chair balanced and keep it from tipping or flipping over.

One thing I get asked almost every time I talk about wheelchair tennis to an able-bodied person is how I wheel while holding a tennis racket or whether I use a power chair. I explain that power chairs are not permitted and would not be effective. You also want your sport chair to be as lightweight as possible because the less amount of weight you have, the easier and faster you can move. I explain about sport chairs, but understandably they look quite dubious.

Since I had such an extensive tennis background, I figured any learning curve would be small. After all, how hard could it be? I was quickly disabused of this notion, and with a little trepidation, I went out to the court and gingerly sat in the wheelchair.

The chair was missing some screws, the tires were flat, and I had no idea what I was doing, but I loved it from the first minute I tried it.

It didn't look like it would be too challenging, and I figured once I got the hang of it, I would be fine. I have since learned that although there isn't much difference in rules or the basic premise, wheelchair and able-bodied tennis are two completely different sports.

Once I had a tennis wheelchair and a very basic first lesson, I headed to Barnes Tennis Center in Point Loma, California.

After unloading my chair, wheels, and tennis racket, I attempted to cart it all through the pro shop and down the hill to the tennis courts with my mother assisting.

"Hi, my name is Leslie!"

"Hi, Leslie. I'm Vicky."

Another player, Stan, smiled at me as I tried to assemble my chair. Vicky gave me pointers. I asked about the footplate, which seemed to be at an odd angle, and looked at the straps the others had holding their feet to the footplate.

"Do I need a strap as well?"

"Not unless you need to keep your feet from falling off," Vicky replied.

Since then, I have learned that for me a strap holding my feet is very important. Otherwise, I tend to kick my legs when trying to move.

They were very welcoming and recognized immediately that I was totally lost with no idea what I was doing. They informed me that my chair had flat tires and was in imminent danger of collapsing. After helping me to refill my tires with air and attempting to tighten my screws, they did their best to help me get started. They gave me some basic pointers and went off to warm up together, leaving me to my own devices. My mother helped by feeding me balls, and I did my best to get close enough to hit them.

One of the questions that I had almost immediately was what to do when the ball is coming right at you. Vicki showed me some sort of maneuver that I attempted to replicate with little success. It should have been obvious to me that the answer was to move out of the way and get in a position to hit a

Learning the Basics

backhand or a forehand, but all of this felt so new to me. I understood this concept but still had the deer in the headlights look when the ball was coming right at me, and I couldn't decide quickly enough which way to move. I would end up freezing and either getting hit with the ball or occasionally would manage to hit some pathetic shot. If the ball bounces in the court and hits either you or your wheelchair, you lose the point.

After a while, I was invited to rotate into the doubles that the rest of the group was playing. Quickly they realized that I was unable to play to any level. and the offer of having my mother stand behind me, to hit any of the balls (mostly all of them) that I missed was unappealing.

No one likes to look foolish or athletically inept. I am sure I committed a lot of maneuvers that were totally awkward, but I felt like I'd finally found my sport.

A tactic that is very successful in wheelchair tennis is hitting the ball behind someone. If you pull your opponent off the side of the court, they will move back towards the center after they hit the ball. While they are heading back to the center, you hit the ball to the side of the court that they are currently moving away from.

It is difficult to change direction quickly and effectively enough, especially at my level, to retrieve a ball that you are moving away from. Turning your chair around, moving back to recover, or coming in for a short ball are all important skills, especially in a wheelchair. The way you turn your chair is also quite important. If you're heading to the left and a ball is hit to your right, your first inclination is to turn to the right and start moving that way. However, it is much more effective if you circle around. It is challenging to train your mind to do something that seems almost counterintuitive.

In able-bodied tennis, you learn about a variety of footwork used to reach the ball and get in a good position. Eventually, this becomes ingrained, and you don't have to think about it. It is so much harder in a wheelchair. Although the steps are replicated with wheels, it is much more difficult to maneuver. Especially in a tournament or pressure situation where you revert to what you are most comfortable with, which is often the exact incorrect way.

Spitfire

Many other wheelchair players can play or practice several times a week or for much longer than I can. Although they are disabled, their energy levels are "normal," and they don't struggle as much with fatigue. At one of the last tournaments I attended, my friend Melissa said she had played an extra set with some players she knew after the match play was over, for fun. The thought of that was inconceivable to me.

BASIC TRAINING

In October of 2018 and 2019 I attended All Comers wheelchair tennis camp in Florida. It's a three-day camp, and it consists of drills, with a lot of mini matches and exercises consisting of winning points and rotating.

The first year I went, I was very apprehensive, especially about how I would be able to keep up. Two hours is a lot of tennis for me; how was I supposed to do two and a half days, especially back-to-back?

Surprisingly, I was able to keep up, despite the long days, the fast pace, and the fact that it was over 90 degrees and very humid. Every time we stopped to have a discussion, share information, explain new drills, or even wait in line, all the players gravitated to the side of the court where there was shade.

Each day we stopped for lunch, and then all met in the evening for a group dinner. It's great to be able to get to know the other players and learn so much in a short time. It was one of the coaches in 2018 that hooked me up with someone who could help me size, order, and purchase a sport chair. I met a lot of new people and enjoyed reconnecting with people I'd met at tournaments.

The second year was as amazing as the first but different. I knew a lot of the people, and it was fun to be back together. The second day it rained, so instead of playing, we had a group lecture. It focused on strategies for a match in terms of recovering from a bad shot or lost game, as well as how to use the time on the crossover to eat, hydrate, and prepare for the next game. Since so much of tennis is a mental game, strategy is essential.

We covered the topic of how "self-talk" and body language can affect your performance and the outcome of a match. Having information about how to put your best foot forward and to have as much advantage as possible is what makes this camp so important, but it also makes for a lot of fun and laughs.

BECOME ONE WITH THE CHAIR

One of the first things I was told about wheelchair tennis was that the more connected you are with your chair and the more it becomes an extension of your body, the better your movement will be. I have two disadvantages when it comes to being one with my chair. First, I suffer from pervasive fatigue, which means the longer a match goes the more my movement suffers. Movement, or lack of movement, is one of the most important things in tennis. The second is that I (fortunately, in some ways) don't use a wheelchair on a daily basis, so I have much less experience than those who are in a wheelchair 24/7.

The ease and comfort that someone has who is always in a chair is much more advanced than someone who isn't. Strengths such as maneuverability can make a big difference. I've been told that at some point, I won't have to think about moving the chair as I once didn't have to think about moving my feet, and the chair will, in essence, become my feet. Getting to that point would be a huge improvement as there are so many different things I'm trying to remember what to do at each point, which means I inevitably forget some.

Another invaluable piece of advice that I received several times is to "always keep the chair moving." Whenever I asked other players for their advice or was getting a critique, this was pointed out to me again and again. Whatever else you are doing during a match, if you're not keeping your chair moving continually, you aren't going to win.

For me, my movement is the hardest part of the game. I have adjusted, in some ways, to playing in a wheelchair versus not.

I've had to transition from a two-handed backhand to a one-handed backhand, so it isn't as hard or as accurate. I have had to adopt a more western grip on the racket, so my grip has changed to between a forehand and backhand grip. I have more power since I have been taping my hand, but it's nowhere close to the power I had in my prime. All these changes make it a completely different game from the way I previously played tennis, even more than the transition from my feet to my chair. The longer I play, and the more I improve, the clearer the fact that wheelchair tennis and able-bodied tennis are two completely different games. While there are many similarities, the whole outlook and strategy are very modified and make my previous knowledge and expertise much less of an advantage.

I still have the strokes, the understanding of the game and the format, and all the knowledge and skills from playing for many years. However, if my movement isn't good enough to get me to the ball, the best strokes in the world wouldn't matter. Another adjustment that I'm trying to make is to hit the ball while I'm still moving. This is yet another concept that I'm working on grasping.

To aid in improving my movement, I have used any opportunity to work on my upper body strength and build the appropriate muscles by rolling. A significant stumbling block is that I seem to think my chair is moving even when it isn't. The more focused I am on other parts of the game, the more I tend to stop. This seems to occur the most when I get exhausted.

It is also important to work on building up the calluses on your hands so you don't have to deal with large amounts of blisters and friction burns. If I haven't played for a while, I can feel my hands burning just a few minutes in. If your hands are hurting, that makes it even more difficult to have good movement because rolling makes it much worse.

I don't like to buy big ticket items, such as a sports wheelchair until I determine that it is something I am sure I want to do and will be invested in using. I started out with a borrowed chair for a few days in California that was, to be blunt, a piece of crap with missing screws and wobbly tires. The second chair I rented for a month from Vermont Adaptive Sports was better, but not much. The seat wasn't the right size, and my toes were hitting the ground, which caused me to use my toes to push, which is not a habit I wanted to form. Think of it like different pairs of shoes. The first pair was beaten up and falling apart. The second pair was better because they were still intact, and although they didn't fit, they were better than nothing. The third chair I borrowed was a great chair that I used for over a year and fit well.

Finally, I purchased a perfect chair that was fitted for me and was basically custom-built. Rather than a thigh strap which I previously had, I have a waistband, which helps me to stay in and connected to my chair. But once I have it on, I can't reach the ground to pick up balls or anything else. Having ball runners on the court is helpful since they pick up the balls. Added on to the fact that I have a racket taped to my hand I need a lot of assistance at times.

In addition to the price of a chair, there are also wheels, which require pumps, bags to travel, spare tires and tubes (the part that goes in the wheels), as well as rackets, tennis bags, and other equipment. All of this can add up. However, I knew that this opportunity to be a wheelchair tennis player would change my life and make it possible for me to be involved in the tennis world again.

TOURNAMENTS

I have had several matches in wheelchair tennis that are lengthy, some that are close to three hours, often because I win the first set. I start to struggle during the second set and often end up losing that, even if I have a lead at the start of the set. By the time the third set rolls around, I am out of steam and am in no position to play. I do everything I can to no avail. I hit a wall, and although I can force myself to go on, I have less than empty in my fuel tank.

In 2018 at my second tournament, which I won, I was playing in the B flight. I won so many points, I became the #1 ranked B player!

When I got a call from the tournament director of the Cajun Classic in 2019, a few days before the tournament I realized the downside of being ranked #1. She informed me that since I was ranked so high, I would now have to play in the A flight, a place I had no business being. This contributed to me losing almost all the matches I played in 2019, which was not all that surprising. Since my ranking dropped quite a bit, I could then go back to playing in the B flight. Unfortunately, the pandemic hit a few days before the Cajun Classic 2020. Although most of the tournaments have opened up, I haven't wanted to travel, stay in a hotel or play in any indoor facilities.

COMPETITIVE EDGE

In October 2017, I attended my first wheelchair tennis tournament in Chicago and got a taste of competing in wheelchair tennis. This was a great tournament to start with because it was small and informal. When I registered for this tournament, I was hoping to play in the women's C flight but soon realized that there was no such thing. My mom tried to discourage me from going since I hadn't been playing long. However, I was ready to try my new skills and excited to learn more about the sport, especially because I didn't have any local community to experience.

At breakfast on the first day, I met some players who were able to find my match in the schedule. I found out that my match wasn't until 5 PM that afternoon, but decided to go to the site, register, and get acclimated. While waiting for the tournament van at the hotel, I met more players and felt like I was already starting to make connections. Everyone was very welcoming, and it was easy to strike up a conversation with anyone, including players, coaches, or companions.

My first match was a bit disappointing (I still have the mindset that I'm a winner at everything, even if I have no idea what I'm doing). I was constantly moving forward when I needed to go backward, continually in the wrong place, and it looked and felt like it was my first time. Which it was. Although Michaela and I have become good friends and doubles partners, I still haven't beaten her. She showcased one of her best and most challenging shots, continually high-looping balls that went over my head, and if I managed to get them back, it was followed by a drop shot. I'm sure I spent a lot of time not moving and when I was moving, it was usually in the wrong direction. I just continued trying to do the best I could, but it was a bit of a lost cause. Still, I was happy to be playing tennis again and considered it a learning experience, despite my competitive nature.

Surprisingly enough, I wasn't nervous before this match or at this tournament, maybe because it was so small and very unintimidating, but most likely because I had no idea what I was doing or what to expect. I was excited and a little apprehensive, as I am in most new situations.

The next morning, which happened to be my birthday, I was scheduled to play Emily at 8 AM. We arrived at the site early, and my mother and I went out on the courts to warm up with a lot of other players.

This was what I'd been hoping to find, a community and collaborative spirit of a group of people all in the same boat, or at least on the same ocean. I was looking forward to competing and being competitive but was also hoping to find a group of people that I could become part of. To some extent, this was the case, especially at such a small tournament. The openness and willingness to help others was something that I wasn't used to in my previous able-bodied competitions.

The outcome of my second match was an improvement, as I won a set. Unfortunately, this was to become a pattern that has continued. As often happens, my energy was gone, and the third set (a 10-point tiebreaker) was completely downhill. Sometimes, when I overexert myself, I tend to experience a drop in my cognitive functioning ability as well. This match was over three hours long, and I had burned through every drop of energy I had. Thinking clearly requires energy, and I had even run out of fumes. During the tiebreaker, I continually forgot the score, and it was a bit surreal and before I knew it the match was over.

What I came to realize now is that I cannot sustain any high level of playing for more than an hour or so. If I'm in a long match, it is more likely that I am going to lose. Three hours was way too long.

PART SEVEN

DEUCE

DEUCE

Deuce in a tennis match occurs when both players have "40" and can also be called "40 all." This is a point when there is equilibrium between opponents. For either person to win the game, they must win two consecutive points. If a player wins one point but loses the second, it reverts to deuce and equilibrium is once again restored. In life, (especially as a Libra), we are always seeking equilibrium, a balance where the scales are equal, and neither one is lesser or greater than the other. The scales continually go up and down, sometimes dramatically, sometimes only a little, until they again reach a state of balance. This state is very tenuous, and any small action can cause a transfer, throwing balance off again.

POSITIVE AND COMPETITIVE

"Regardless of your competition or circumstances, ask yourself only to do your best, as this is all you can do." (The Champion's Mind, pg. 81)

In a tennis match you are not only playing your opponent on the other side of the net, but you are also playing with, or against, yourself and your own mind. Whether you are playing singles or doubles, there is only yourself to count on; therefore, your mind game is one the most important factors.

Confidence can cause you to win a match even if you are playing an opponent that is better than you. Lack of confidence can cause you to lose to someone who is not as strong a player as you. In effect, your mind can help or hinder you, and it is important to use your mind as a tool, rather than as a handicap.

Your attitude about a match can make all the difference. If you approach the match with the belief that you can win, it will help you play to the best of your ability. Conversely, self-defeating thoughts or a pessimistic outlook can cause a self-fulfilling prophecy. Your belief in yourself and your abilities isn't going to win the match, but it will make it possible to do your best. When you play to win, there is a much greater chance of that occurring.

I play to win every day in every area of my life. Just as mental toughness is necessary in the sporting arena, it is also essential for a positive and productive life.

I do my best every single day, whatever my best looks like on any given day. I choose the positive over the negative and use mental toughness to find happiness, despite my struggles. I always try to find the silver lining, to find the sun amidst the clouds. To remind me that when the forecast is partly cloudy, it means that it is also partly sunny. Being mentally tough just means always striving to use a strengths-based perspective and having a positive slant and an optimistic outlook.

Spitfire

There are days when I am unable to be mentally tough. My mind frame is negative, and my lack of positivity brings me down to where my perspective is bleak and life seems hopeless. All I can do is allow myself to have these feelings, let them go, and remember that tomorrow is another day. Eventually, I can find my confidence and am able to return to a positive, optimistic framework.

The empathy and compassion I bring to each day help me to find my way, especially in times of darkness, and by doing so, I find my joy. Empathy and compassion are core parts of me and make me who I am. These attributes also help me to remain in a positive frame of mind because it gives me a purpose. It also gives me energy, all of which contribute to my sense of well-being.

There is an old Cherokee legend that has always been one of my favorite analogies of the way to find a happy and joyful life. A grandfather explains to his young grandson that there are two wolves within us. One wolf is positive and beneficial, and the other wolf is negative and destructive. These two wolves are constantly battling against each other for control over us. The grandson asks his grandfather, "Which one will win?" and the grandfather replies, "The one you feed." When I remember to feed the positive wolf and express empathy and compassion for others, I can also feel empathy and compassion for myself.

EMPATHY & COMPASSION

In my case, empathy and compassion work wonders, while sympathy and pity make everything worse. I am well acquainted with what my situation is, and when others point out, "wow, you have a hard life," "it must be so hard," or "how can you do it," etc. my initial response is an indignant "that's right, I do have a hard life, my life is so challenging." This attitude will get me nowhere fast except into a pity spiral. I can't live my life the way I want to if I spend all my time feeling oh so sorry for myself. There is nothing wrong with sitting with the sadness of my unfortunate situation, and it can be an important thing to do, but melting into a little puddle in the corner isn't going to make anything better.

There are times when I do feel sorry for myself, but this is the natural course of life; everyone feels sorry for themselves at times. You can get stuck in the quagmire of pity and indignation, or you can get back on your feet, dust yourself off, and move on. Dissolving isn't my style, and I'd much rather focus on the glass having some water in it than the fact that it is not even half full.

The anger and sadness that I feel regarding my health can only be counteracted by forward motion, which to me, is everything. There are days and times when I struggle to rise above the notion that everything is hopeless, so I might as well set up permanent residence in my bed and exist on potato chips and popcorn. This, I know from experience, occurs when I am utterly and completely exhausted, overwhelmed by life's challenges, and need to get out of town, get warm, get rested, and recharge.

In this space, I can turn to anger, and the minute I feel a spark of anger, my first thought is about finding which destructive pattern I can immediately use to cope. Unfortunately, my go-to pattern is eating, which starts the vicious cycle of eating because I feel angry, and which transfers to being angry about my eating. This is a continuous cycle of around and around and around until I find a way to release myself. Otherwise, I am fighting a losing battle that is only going to make the future more difficult.

By continuing to put one foot in front of the other, I move in a positive direction. The landscape changes as I go, which contributes to making the journey interesting, with new and exciting experiences right around the next corner, and I am no longer stuck and can continue slogging through the mud of depression.

Having a disease, which causes your muscles to deteriorate, creates a situation in that you are sliding backward even while you are continuing to work on moving forward. As for standing still, that is basically throwing in the towel and giving up any hope of maintaining what you currently have.

I look for those in my life who can reinforce and support my feeling of continuing to move forward rather than those who look at me with pity and dismay and suggest that I might as well give up. Just as I am more than willing to take any positives that I can from having a disability, I want to be treated and seen as everyone's equal rather than pitied. But you can't have it both ways. You can't use the resources or assistance afforded to a disabled person and then not be labeled as disabled or not be ok or accept being seen as a disabled person. This contradiction is at the forefront of my every thought, ever apparent to me, almost becoming a symptom of my disability.

It is hard for me to take assistance, and I find myself fighting against myself; for example, going skiing with friends and wanting to carry my own skis even though someone offered to carry them. These were people who did not know that I had any physical disabilities, and I wanted to keep it that way. So, I carry them and end up falling and getting hurt. Lately, it has become easier for me to let others do things for me, but I still struggle with the fine line between someone helping and me appearing less than able. I must be able to see the difference between my husband assisting me with something that is difficult for me to do or him "taking care of me" and doing things for me that I could easily do myself. Sometimes he can do something easier or faster than I can. Knowing I have a finite amount of energy, he was willing to get something from upstairs or downstairs, driving me, or doing an errand so that I didn't have to. I like him doing favors for me, and he is good about not making me feel guilty for this.

I am not asking for others to not see me as disabled; I am just asking not to be pitied. In my work with developmentally disabled (DD) adults, I have witnessed their desire to be viewed as "normal," and "equal." I watched a documentary about DD adults whose theme surrounded showcasing how "normal" they are. However, if they were, in fact, "normal," then no one would be interested in doing a documentary about them, and no one would want to see one if they did. It is hard to be seen as "other" or "different," especially during adolescence when everyone wants to fit in. My goal is to help those I work with realize that they are who they are and they are not what is viewed by the general population as "normal." But in the end, who is "normal," and what does it even mean? Normal is just a social construction that leads some to feel that they qualify and others to feel outside. The desire to be "normal" is the desire to feel commonality, normalcy, and comradery with others. We are all different and unique in our own ways. It takes all varieties to make up a world.

I embody compassion and need compassion in return. Compassion helps me to continue to fight the good fight and to feel the power of doing all I can every day. I do want sympathy, as well as empathy, but not in the-sky-is-falling, and the-world-is-ending sort of way. Yeah, it's tough, and I get down about my situation, very down. When I attempt to do things that I could easily do just a few short years ago, I feel a flush of sadness. When I have a fun day snowshoeing with a friend and find I can't get out of bed the next day because I overdid it, I feel anger. When I use the phrase "I can't," I cringe inside.

What I need to learn to do is not to compare myself. Not only not to others but to who I used to be or who I was. I need to compare myself to who I want to be and become and use that vision to guide me forward. When I can't make my body do what I want it to do, it can be somewhere between annoying and completely devastating.

It is what it is, and crying over it won't change anything. There are those days when I can't compete against myself, and my bootstraps break as I try to pull myself up. In everyone's life, there are those times. Nobody has it easy all the time. I try to remember that we all have our struggles, and no one can really know what another's life is like. We can walk in someone else's shoes by using empathy and compassion as a tool to ease their way, but not to make it harder. There but for the grace of God go I.

PASSION

My family has always been big believers in nontraditional medicine, and since there was relatively nothing the doctors or conventional medicine could do to help us, we were more than willing to try alternative routes. The loss of energy was one of the symptoms that we found the most challenging. To this end, In 2001, we decided to consult an energy worker.

Walking up the steps of an old brownstone, I felt hopeful about my appointment with an energy worker that my mother had found. An energy worker might be an answer to the intense amount of fatigue I had been battling. If nothing else, she couldn't make it any worse! I didn't have a lot of information about the Russian energy worker I was on my way to meet but was willing to try anything. I knew about chi, life force, and getting energy from the universe. I was hoping she could help and was hoping I could find a way to siphon some of the excess energy that my boyfriend had.

What I mostly remember are snippets of our conversation. She talked about different ways of getting energy from the universe, that I couldn't take anyone else's energy and not to shower for several hours after the appointment, or it would somehow wash off the effects.

Getting energy from the universe means a variety of different things, but one of the things that I remember her emphasizing was about being able to get energy from the passion in our lives.

Passion, I have come to realize, is one of the single most important elements of finding joy and meaning in life. If you can find your passion, and you must, in order to thrive and survive, you can find a way to make it through whatever you are struggling against. The passion I have for the beach is easy to fulfill, and without that refuge and connection, there would be a great void in my life.

A close second is tennis. Tennis was a huge part of my identity and when I was no longer able to play, I lost so much more than just an activity. Finding wheelchair tennis brought a sense of community, and the ability to return to something that I not only loved but was a part of my soul has been paramount.

For those of us living in a compromised situation, it is vital to find something we are passionate about. Without this, there is no reason to get up in the morning. Passions are different for everyone. For my brother, it is disabled sailing. He is passionate about sailing and was no longer able to do it without adaptation. Sailing is in his blood and in his soul, and no matter how tired or discouraged he is, he can always rise to the occasion, and I believe, like tennis for me, that sailing has saved his life.

I cannot emphasize this enough. If you know what you are passionate about, embrace it fully. If not, determine the activity that fills you, makes you smile, and makes your life a little bit brighter and worth living. It is the only way to have a full and satisfactory life. You can see someone's whole demeanor change when they are engaged in something they are passionate about.

I only had one appointment with the energy worker and hadn't noticed any difference, although it probably takes more than one session for any effects to be felt. My energy has continued to decrease, but I have been able to draw on the energy of the universe by focusing on my passions and trying to eliminate from my life the things that deplete my energy rather than add to it.

HOPE & FAITH

"I have always experienced Leslie as having quite a 'hope floats,' a resiliency..." – Peggy Sax

Through all the trials and tribulations I have gone through, I have always had hope. It is said that our lives are caught between the opposing forces of hope and fear and that these two emotions are the ones that create the decisions we make and our everyday actions. Fear is an easy enough emotion to understand and to see how it drives and directs us. Hope is a much more complex concept.

Hope is possible to see at work every day. People that have lived through devastating natural disasters such as Katrina, the earthquake in Haiti, the tsunami in Japan, President Trump, and COVID have shown incredible amounts of hope. It is hope that makes us get up in the morning and to keep going, especially in the face of incredible loss and insurmountable obstacles. It is hope, not fear, that motivates me. Even as fear is the flip side of hope, while feeling incredible hope, there is no place for fear.

In the end, hope is all we have. The hope that things will change, that things will get better, that I can beat the encroaching onslaught of my disability. Hope for a new day and a brighter future. Hope is filled with light and optimism; fear is cold, dark, and filled with despair. All situations can be looked at from either a place of fear or a place of hope. Fear that if I don't get up I never will, or hope that today will be a better or easier day.

This is where faith and spirituality come in. My faith and religion are closely bound to a mix of many ideas, beliefs, and practices. Faith is deeply personal and highly complicated. My feelings of faith and the beliefs that I hold are very important to me and have gotten me through some very tough places.

I believe in angels and the power of positive thought. I believe in the power and energy of the universe, karma, and that everything we do in life will come back around. I use that belief to assist me in living a life that helps others rather than makes life harder for them. If I don't use my gifts, then they will be wasted, and maybe in my next life, I won't have any gifts to give. I don't know if there is reincarnation, the afterlife, or hell, but I know that this one life can't be the end of everything.

My idea of heaven is a place where you can lay in the sun on the beach all day and not get a sunburn or skin cancer, where you can run and swim and dance and play and never get tired. A place where you sleep only to have fantastic dreams, but not because you need rest, and movement of any sort is effortless.

Everything that I long for in life is possible in my heaven. After all, it is my dream. I can run for miles and dance all night in ridiculously high heels. My thighs never rub together, so I can wear skirts as much as I want. My stomach is flat, and my chest is small, so I can wear sexy, skimpy tops. I have long, thick, wavy hair. I know none of these things are anything other than fantasy, and I am not foolish enough to believe that any of these attributes would actually be all I need to be happy. I have learned that it is incorrect to believe that if you only had a specific thing or didn't have something, that you would be happy and fulfilled.

JOY

"...When you sense a faint potentiality for happiness after such dark times, you must grab onto the ankles of that happiness and not let go until it drags you face-first out of the dirt— this is not selfishness but obligation." (Gilbert, 115)

Two of my favorite concepts are joy and happiness. The key elements of joy and happiness are health, wealth, friendship/companionship, and whatever each of these elements mean to us. Without any of these elements, it is quite challenging for happiness and joy to be the result. I can say at this point that my health is much challenged, and my wealth is very minimal. I do have wonderful friendships, family, and people in my life that bring me joy. I don't feel that I am missing any of the key elements, although others may argue that I struggle with two out of three.

Health is not just physical health but healthy relationships, healthy attitude, or, conversely, unhealthy situations. Wealth can be about so much more than money. It can be wealth of happiness or love, wealth of friends or family or other areas of life that can be so much more important and fulfilling than cold, hard cash. It is the outlook and perspective you have, where you are coming from and where you hope to be going that is more important than having perfect health and all the wealth you could desire.

In essence, it is about your state of mind. "But without the right mental attitude, without attention to the mental factor, these things have very little impact on our long-term feelings of happiness." (Dalai Lama, Cutler 25)

The mental factor is where I struggle. It is where all my doubts, anxieties, fears, emotions, and thoughts that detract from my happiness are. By learning about enlightenment, I hope I will gain an understanding that will help me to find happiness easier to attain. I feel that having learned that it is more a place to be rather than just an emotion causes it to become less elusive and more an area that I can have access to. It follows that something that helps us gain this mental state can be very useful in finding a calmness and peacefulness in our minds.

Another source of happiness is the feeling of self-worth, an internal factor that I have greatly struggled with. Having a positive feeling of self-worth is something that became harder and harder for me to have as my body, which I grew up viewing as my best asset, began to fail me again and again. I have had times of such low levels or lack of self-esteem that it led me to have complete disregard for myself. How could I be happy with a complete lack of self-worth?

My self-worth is an area that is improving and growing as I begin to find my place in the world and follow what is important to me. Such as finding and cultivating people, places, and activities that bring me happiness and joy.

I believe that there is a direct correlation between the value that you place on yourself and your level of contentment. That idea is no stretch at all. If you are continually unhappy and disappointed by yourself, then there is no hope of contentment. I don't mean contentment, as in there is nothing more you need to do, work on, or improve. I mean feeling that you are moving forward in the right direction and that you are doing your part to make the world a better and happier place rather than adding to the misery. That is what contentment is all about to me.

The tenor of our culture tells us that if we can't find happiness, then pleasure can be a substitute. As a culture, we are hedonistic and pleasure-seeking. If it feels good, or makes us feel better, why on earth would we not do it?

Along with pleasure, we want instant gratification. Who cares about the long run or the big picture? I want what I want, and I want it now. I continually wondered how, if I am doing all these things that are supposed to make me feel good, why do I feel so bad? Why am I so damn unhappy? As consumers, we feel it is our right to buy the things we want and covet. Whether or not we need them is immaterial.

I have found that when I have bought things just because I want them or to make myself happy, I end up with buyer's remorse. It is along the same lines as if I were thinner, I would be happy; or my belief in my 20s that if I had a boyfriend, I would be happy. The only problem is once I would lose weight or find a relationship, I would still be unhappy because I had only changed the exterior and hadn't changed myself at all. That is what my present journey is all about.

Rather than a journey to somewhere external, it is an internal journey to determine who I am, what I need, and what I can do to be the person I want and am striving to be.

Receiving a graduate degree and moving to Colorado helped me to slow down and change my perspective. But as I learned much earlier on, you can run, but you can't hide. Wherever you go, there you are. Although these changes may help, the thing that really needed to change was me. I stopped running and slowed down long enough to realize that if I only have one life to live, then I needed to make some significant changes and use the discoveries I made to shape the life I wanted. In all the teachings I have studied, the best way to become what and who you want to be is to start cultivating that persona. Start living life the way you want your life to be, and eventually, you will be that person. Love the life you live and live the life you love.

I am on a journey and trying to find some signposts that will lead me in the direction that I want to go in. When I find things that resonate with what I am doing or thinking, it increases my feeling that I am on the right track and that I am getting closer to finding the path I want to be traveling on. No matter the twist and turns, hills and valleys, forks, obstacles, rough terrain, and, inevitably, the setbacks. When I am on the path that is right for me, it won't be as difficult to travel despite the strength I will need. It will feel right, and there will be less to struggle against since I will no longer be fighting against the current and trying to swim upstream...as I have for so much of my life. The more encouragement I give myself, and the stronger my belief in my own power becomes, the more of the fog clears from the road.

One way to help determine what will make me happy in this world and life is to ask that simple question, "will it make me happy." I need to look at situations in a way that will help me determine whether my action or lack thereof will make me happy or not. Making the decision based on what will make me the happiest would be helpful in making positive choices.

Spitfire

Another part of that equation is what will make me the happiest for the longest amount of time or what may make me marginally unhappy right now, but will, in the end, cause me great joy.

TRANSITION

There is a brightness to my life that breaks through like the sun through the clouds and makes me smile and sing along to the songs on the radio. The current burden I face is how to determine what path to take at this juncture and how to come to terms with the reality of my unexpected life and what this newly defined life will look like. To move on, these burdens must be faced and overcome, or I will constantly dwell in a place of uncertainty, turning to antidepressants and any narcotics that can be used for recreation and oblivion, or at the very least, a change in perspective.

Reality must be faced, and finding a new, clear perspective is what my ongoing journey is about. While I try not to let the tides of depression drown me, I look for a way to forge ahead and use my introspection to lead me.

Once, in describing to my mother my struggle with depression, I used an ocean metaphor: "I feel like I am in the water and there are huge waves rushing at me, one after the other. I keep getting dragged under and tumbled around until I finally reach the surface. As soon as I get my feet under me, another huge wave crashes over me, and I have to fight all over again."

Although I felt like this was a clear description, my mother looked at me in puzzlement. "Why don't you just get out of the water?"

This thought had never occurred to me. I thought my only option was to fight and fight and struggle and do the best I could to keep my head above the water. I came to understand that I was fighting and struggling against myself. I realized that I could only depend on myself to get rescued. I had to find a way out of the water on my own. That was the only way to get out of the water and onto dry land.

My situation just plain sucks. That is a pure and simple fact. I think often about the opportunities I didn't have that I would have liked to have, the opportunities that I took in an effort not to miss anything and strenuously wished I had missed, and all the other things I may have missed out on. It is valid and necessary to state all these thoughts, feelings, ideas, and issues about how angry, pissed off, and in some ways, regretful I feel.

When I was finally ready to start "dealing" with my diagnosis, I was already feeling some of the detrimental symptoms and effects. I was so busy fighting against this diagnosis that it took me years to be able to work with it and do the things that would help my body and myself and make things easier.

There is only living this life, bearing up every day and accomplishing tasks that seem insurmountable. How do I find my joy, when I am spending my time soldiering forward and trying to keep a low profile, holding my muscles tight, and not daring to relax for fear it will all just stop? Not the struggle, just me. The struggle will continue.

I know from experience that this, too, shall pass. From being clinically depressed and convinced that overwhelming darkness is how I will feel for the rest of my life, I did recover. It seemed to happen while I was busy doing other things.

I want to be the master and the director, the alpha and the omega, of my own life and my own journey. I don't want to leave everything up to the winds of fate. There is the belief that if you ask the universe for something, it will come to you if you open yourself up to all possibilities. I do own this journey; it is mine and becomes what I make of it. The deepest desire that I have is to make it spectacular because I believe there is the possibility for that, and maybe that is my passion.

The most empirical part is to determine what it is that I want, be able to name it, be able to clearly define it, and have it outlined with statements and tenets. After all, how can I find and get what I want if I can't ask for it?

I have finally stopped looking for my happiness and fulfillment through others and know it is not up to them to give me what I want or to make me happy. That must come from within. Although support is essential and helpful and gives me someone to lean into when the wind blows, this journey is elementally my own. I need a way to bridge the gap from where I am to where I am going, from wanting and not receiving, to finding a life, a reality, and a resolution that I can

Transition

live with and ends up looking a lot like what I envision myself having.

I need to stop trying to fix it, trying to push my way through, without the right tools and nothing to help except for my sheer determination and the fact that I can't stop, or else I will never reach the other side.

I do the best I can with the gifts and the strengths that I have to fight my daily struggles in life. The shortest way home is often the longest way around.

MOVING FORWARD

"Never, ever, ever give up." ~Winston Churchill

How do I move forward in a way that is positive, joyful, and peaceful? Perhaps this is the lifelong journey I will be on, to find and learn and relearn the answers. To determine a way to achieve a life that I feel is fully worth living. To find the balance, I am seeking.

In Anne Morrow Lindbergh's collection of diaries and letters "Bring me a unicorn," she states in her introduction the reason to publish letters and diaries: "One wants to be an honest witness to the life one has lived and the struggle one has made to find oneself and one's work and to relate oneself to others and the world." (Lindbergh, xvi) I have the desire to use what I have learned and to examine the struggles I have faced and some of the lessons I have learned along the way. I want to use what I have experienced to help me to understand my life and who I am inside, how I got to where I am, and most of all, to do it honestly.

To look at my life honestly and objectively at the same time is indeed a challenge. Having a disease is not who or what I am but something that is a part of me that I live with every day and has, in many ways, shaped me. It has played a role in developing who I am and who I will become and reinforced the necessity of examining where I am, where I want to go, and how in this present state, I can begin to move in that direction. I want to have this journey culminate in a place where I can use all my skills to relate to others in the world we all cohabitate. "In terms of the individual, there is a wish to give testimony to a journey taken by one human being which might amuse, enlighten, or explain other individuals to themselves." (Lindbergh xv) This is my goal, my fondest wish, which I continually express. If I can use my writing as a way to help others bear the pain of their journey, I will have succeeded. I not only want to be a light in the darkness but to lighten the darkness for others.

It is comforting to know that others have walked the same or similar path as you and survived. There is a feeling of validation that comes from someone else walking in your shoes or at least having a similar taste in footwear. My goal is to relate to the world at large and in the process, learn to relate inward, honestly, fiercely, and fearlessly.

There is no reason or point to share my story, my thoughts, feelings, and ideas if not to help support others; especially those who may have to go this way alone, without support or the strength of others to lean on. Above all, to anyone and everyone who has ever had to struggle in a sharply altered world or has endured a crisis of faith in themselves, or, in essence, for everyone.

Writing this and researching different books has changed my life so completely. I have grown and changed through this process and have ended up in a place that is the polar opposite in some ways from where I began. This experience has helped me to define many things in my life, what I want, what I need, who I am, and what is important to me.

I have been able to take hard situations and find ways to make them easier to bear and to live with every day. Not knowing what the future holds, especially in terms of my disease advancing, is scary and anxiety producing, but I am more able to focus on the here and now, release old hurts, injustices, and angers, regrets and mistakes, and go from here, to wherever here is and take each day as the gift that it is.

We all have influential and special people in our lives who give us the courage and the strength to go on. It is these people, their stories, testimonies, or thoughts, that help and give us direction. When I find words of others that speak to me, it lends images and pathways for my own understanding and gives me a way to tell the stories that are important to me.

I will make my mark, change the world, and leave, if nothing else, at least one person's life changed for the better. That is my goal, to be a light, a beacon, a strength, or at least a slight comfort to those who are on a similar journey to mine but do not have the ability to see out of the blackness. And maybe I can be a leader for them, as others have been for me.

CONCLUSION

"Leslie has a way of tapping into her own dreams, like writing this book and having projects, and taking charge of her life. And shaping her life in certain ways having a sense of agency." ~Peggy Sax

Looking back 11 years ago to when I started this journey of writing, I was a very different person than I am today. I have moved from a place of anger and depression to a place of acceptance and peace. I used writing to gain understanding and insight of how to begin healing. The thoughts and words poured out of me, and I realized that there was a lot of work and discovery I needed to do. I had to embark on a journey to find and shape a life that I was willing to live.

There were several things that occurred and changed over the years that have led me to the place where I have the ability and energy to look back clearly and explore who I am, what I want and how to get there.

First, I needed to find someone to help guide me through the anger and fear in order to make any kind of life possible. To this end, I began to find a different lens through which to view what seemed to be a life existing entirely in the darkness. Learning the skill of giving myself a break was imperative, although challenging. If I couldn't do something I previously could or was struggling, I would castigate myself. Clearly, this didn't make the situation, circumstances, or outcome any better, but it was my go-to on how to deal with what I considered to be my underperforming.

Eventually, I was fortunate enough to have the means to be able to stop working and no longer had to drag my exhausted body through day after day, which was continually causing me to be sick and too exhausted to do anything except spend most of my days and all my weekends in bed from the moment I got home.

Working on this writing project, first with my best friend, then on my own, and eventually with my best friend again, continued to give me joy and fortification. Being at the beach, at the ocean, and smelling salt air is a passion. Starting wheelchair tennis and engaging in a competitive sport that I loved and was good at fueled my passion.

Returning to tennis, which I thought would never be possible, helped me to regain a sense of myself and my identity that I had lost. It gave me time to take a breath and use my limited amount of energy to do the things I wanted to do. The ability to dictate how I used my resources.

Having these important pieces of myself return helped to keep my fear, anxiety, and depression around the continuing and worsening symptoms of my disease at bay. I can see, constantly, if not daily, the ravages that are the calling card of MMD. Acceptance of an altered life needs to be reached again and again as my muscles continue to disintegrate and new challenges become a part of daily life.

Battling a disease that affects every part of my body, muscles, cognitive function, and ability to be independent makes it even more important that I draw strength from the physical, social and intellectual activities that nourish me.

Without finding my passion and the things that feed my soul, I may not have been able to reach this point. Finding your passion, whatever it may be, is what makes this journey called life the best it can be.

> *"You need to know your passion and do it because even with this disease, if you find your passion, you can have a full life."*
> -Gail Smith

EPILOGUE

I'm on Good Harbor beach, one of my favorite places in the world. No matter what is going on in my life, the beach always centers me and makes me happy. Good harbor beach has always been a constant in my life.

As I sit on the beach, enjoying the feel of the sun on my skin and watching the waves rolling into shore, I see a young girl walking down the beach with her father. I'm reminded of the day when I sat at the water's edge with my father, and he told me of his recent Myotonic Muscular Dystrophy diagnosis. I remember the fear, confusion, and anxiety I felt as I did my best to make my father laugh. My memory of that day is still crystal clear, and I can see the young woman I was sitting on the beach, whose world was about to crumble.

In the last 22 years, my life has gone up and down many times. From when I first heard of MMD and knew my life was about to change to the total devastation of the doctor's diagnosis to today, when rather than devastated, I feel exhilarated.

The doctors were right about some things, but the loss of dreams and the end of my life as I knew it has never come to pass. My determination, grit, and the fact that I am a spitfire gave me the ability to overcome the death sentence those doctors gave me. The fallout almost did me in, but I never gave up, no matter the odds or how difficult the struggle.

The life I am living today bears little resemblance to that 24-year-old woman, and even less to the 16-year-old girl I was when the first troubling symptoms started to emerge. I am happier than I ever remember being, my self-confidence that I lost so long ago has returned and the future looks bright.

Physically, the symptoms have continued to increase, and my abilities have diminished. But there are hours and even days when I don't feel any disabilities and times when I almost forget that I am any different than any other 46-year-old woman. That is phenomenal.

These days I can make the choice about what I want to focus on. Life isn't all sunshine and lollipops, and this is not a path I ever would have wanted to walk or a journey I could have wished on my worst enemy. There are still a lot of negatives, but now, the positives outweigh them. I never expected to be where I am today, dealing daily with pervasive fatigue, a single woman heading towards my late 40s, and although I wish things could have been different, I have finally reclaimed my life.

Writing this memoir led me to the place I am, and the growth that occurred in the last two years was painful at times, affirming at others and although my marriage ran out of gas along the way, I came back to life. The joy and happiness, the excitement and anticipation that I've found were missing for many years. I realized that the spark inside me hadn't gone out, it was only dormant. Now it is bright and will give me the strength to face the struggles that I will encounter in the future. It is no longer a future I fear but one I can't wait to live and to see what the life I've chosen has in store for me.

APPENDIX

Medical Definitions

Cataract: Cataracts are the clouding of the normally clear lens in the eye. By removing the lens and replacing it with a synthetic lens, it is possible to resume clearer vision.

Defibrillator: Defibrillators are implanted to restore a normal heartbeat by sending an electric shock into the heart. This can be a life-saving method to restart the heart or to help the heart to maintain a normal rhythm.

Echocardiogram: An ultrasound of your heart muscles and valves.

Electrocardiogram (EKG): A test that records the electrical system of your heart. It is painless and done by attaching electrodes to the skin. A pacemaker is read in the same way.

Electrophysiology (EP): A test used to assess your heart's electrical systems and used in the diagnosis of arrhythmias.

Hyaline Membrane: An infant breathing disorder caused by immature lungs. This often occurs in premature newborns and is also called infant repertory distress.

ICD: An implantable cardioverter (see defibrillator).

Myotonia: A symptom of a neuromuscular disorder that causes the delay or inability of muscles to relax or release after they have been contracted.

Myotonic Muscular Dystrophy (MMD) Type 1: A condition characterized by the weakening and wasting of all muscles. There are several different types of MMD, and they can be mild to severe. The age of onset differs between congenital (at birth), adolescent or adult. The later that MMD manifests, the lesser the symptoms arise.

Pacemaker: An implanted device that uses electrical pulses to keep the heart from being too slow or to correct an abnormal rhythm

Pervasive Fatigue: An extreme feeling of tiredness or fatigue, so much so it causes the inability to complete activities of daily living and a decrease of enjoyable activities often leading to depression and/or decreased quality of life

Pleiotropy: A cohort of people with the same diagnosis expressing different symptoms or negative effects.

Preimplantation Genetic Diagnosis (PDD): Testing done an embryo to determine the presence of a specific known genetic disease before it is implanted.

Posttraumatic stress disorder (PTSD): A symptom of experiencing a traumatic event that causes anxiety.

Repeat Length (repeats): Nucleotides are the building blocks of DNA. A "trinucleotide" is a set of three nucleotides. Many genes have repetitive regions but when there are too many repetitions, the gene coding gets disrupted and clinical symptoms may result. Genetic testing can reveal how many of these repeats a person has.

Syncope: Syncope is a feeling of dizziness or passing out due to low blood pressure which causes the heart not to pump enough oxygen to the brain.

VTAC: Ventricular Tachycardia (VTAC) is a very fast heartbeat, which causes an inability for the heart to fill up with blood, which stops flowing. By shocking with a defibrillator, the heartbeat returns to a normal rhythm.

About the Author

Leslie Crocker Smith grew up in two very caring communities: Middlebury, Vermont and Briar Neck, a small enclave on the coast in Gloucester, Massachusetts. Very active and loving competition, Leslie was a natural at sports, horseback riding, playing field hockey, tennis, alpine skiing and figure skating. She competed at Lake Placid in figure skating and had a solo at the college winter carnival each year.

In 2000 at age 25, Leslie was diagnosed with Myotonic Muscular Dystrophy (MMD), an inherited neuro-muscular disease that is progressive and has no cure. This diagnosis caused the end of life as she knew it—and threatened to take away her identity.

Through sheer determination Leslie was able to attend and complete graduate school at the University of Vermont, finding her identity as a social worker, a wheelchair tennis player and a writer. Now 22 years after diagnosis, she continues to inspire others through her determination, her writing and competition in tournaments.

Green Heart Living's mission is to make the world a more loving and peaceful place, one person at a time. Green Heart Living Press publishes inspirational books and stories of transformation, making the world a more loving and peaceful place, one book at a time.

Whether you have an idea for an inspirational book and want support through the writing process—or your book is already written and you are looking for a publishing path—Green Heart Living can help you get your book out into the world.

You can meet Green Heart authors on the Green Heart Living YouTube channel and the Green Heart Living Podcast.

www.GreenHeartLiving.com

Made in the USA
Middletown, DE
23 August 2024

59070136R00113